Table For
Two

D1008375

Jean Paré

www.companyscoming.com
visit our website

Front Cover

1. Sunny Citrus Salads, page 34
2. Pesto-Stuffed Chicken, page 61

Props courtesy of: Pfaltzgraff Canada

Back Cover

1. Chinese BBQ Chicken, page 70
2. Balsamic Soy Turkey, page 68

Props courtesy of: Danesco Inc.

We gratefully acknowledge the following suppliers for their generous support of our Test and Photography Kitchens:

Broil King Barbecues   Hamilton Beach® Canada   Proctor Silex® Canada
Corelle®   Lagostina®   Tupperware®

Table For Two

First Printing February 2009

Library and Archives Canada Cataloguing in Publication
Paré, Jean, date-
Table for two / Jean Paré.
(Original series)
Includes index.
At head of title: Company's coming.
ISBN 978-1-897069-71-4
1. Cookery for two. I. Title. II. Series: Paré, Jean, date–
Original series.
TX652.P378 2009   641.5'612   C2008-903442-2

Published by
Company's Coming Publishing Limited
2311 – 96 Street
Edmonton, Alberta, Canada T6N 1G3
Tel: 780-450-6223   Fax: 780-450-1857
www.companyscoming.com

We acknowledge the financial support of the Government of Canada through the Book Publishing Industry Development Program (BPIDP) for our publishing activities.

Printed in China

Cooking tonight?

A selection of
feature recipes
is only a
click away—
absolutely *FREE!*

Visit us at
www.companyscoming.com

Company's Coming Cookbooks

Original Series

- Softcover, 160 pages
- 6" x 9" (15 cm x 23 cm) format
- Lay-flat plastic comb binding
- Full-colour photos
- Nutrition information

Quick & easy recipes! Everyday ingredients!

Practical Gourmet Series

- Hardcover, 224 pages
- 8" x 10" (21 cm x 26 cm) format
- Full-colour throughout
- Nutrition information

Most Loved Recipe Collection

- Hardcover, 128 pages
- 8 3/4" x 8 3/4" (22 cm x 22 cm) format
- Durable sewn binding
- Full-colour throughout
- Nutrition information

Special Occasion Series

- Softcover, 176 pages
- 8 1/2" x 11" (22 cm x 28 cm) format
- Full-colour throughout
- Nutrition information

See page 157 for more cookbooks.
For a complete listing, visit
www.companyscoming.com

Table of Contents

The Company's Coming Story

Jean Paré (pronounced "jeen PAIR-ee") grew up understanding that the combination of family, friends and home cooking is the best recipe for a good life. From her mother, she learned to appreciate good cooking, while her father praised even her earliest attempts in the kitchen. When Jean left home, she took with her a love of cooking, many family recipes and an intriguing desire to read cookbooks as if they were novels!

"Never share a recipe you wouldn't use yourself."

When her four children had all reached school age, Jean volunteered to cater the 50th anniversary celebration of the Vermilion School of Agriculture, now Lakeland College, in Alberta, Canada. Working out of her home, Jean prepared a dinner for more than 1,000 people, launching a flourishing catering operation that continued for over 18 years. During that time, she had countless opportunities to test new ideas with immediate feedback—resulting in empty plates and contented customers! Whether preparing cocktail sandwiches for a house party or serving a hot meal for 1,500 people, Jean Paré earned a reputation for great food, courteous service and reasonable prices.

As requests for her recipes increased, Jean was often asked the question, "Why don't you write a cookbook?" Jean responded by teaming up with her son, Grant Lovig, in the fall of 1980 to form Company's Coming Publishing Limited. The publication of *150 Delicious Squares* on April 14, 1981 marked the debut of what would soon become one of the world's most popular cookbook series.

The company has grown since those early days when Jean worked from a spare bedroom in her home. Today, she continues to write recipes while working closely with the staff of the Recipe Factory, as the Company's Coming test kitchen is affectionately known.

There she fills the role of mentor, assisting with the development of recipes people most want to use for everyday cooking and easy entertaining. Every Company's Coming recipe is kitchen-tested before it is approved for publication.

Jean's daughter, Gail Lovig, is responsible for marketing and distribution, leading a team that includes sales personnel located in major cities across Canada. Company's Coming cookbooks are distributed in Canada, the United States, Australia and other world markets. Bestsellers many times over in English, Company's Coming cookbooks have also been published in French and Spanish.

Familiar and trusted in home kitchens around the world, Company's Coming cookbooks are offered in a variety of formats Highly regarded as kitchen workbooks, the softcover Original Series, with its lay-flat plastic comb binding, is still a favourite among readers.

Jean Paré's approach to cooking has always called for quick and easy recipes using everyday ingredients. That view has served her well. The recipient of many awards, including the Queen Elizabeth Golden Jubilee Medal, Jean was appointed Member of the Order of Canada, her country's highest lifetime achievement honour.

Jean continues to gain new supporters by adhering to what she calls The Golden Rule of Cooking: *Never share a recipe you wouldn't use yourself.* It's an approach that has worked—millions of times over!

6

Foreword

If you've ever cooked for a small group, you know the challenges. Most recipes are made for four to six servings. So what if there are only two of you? Either you end up with a whole lot of leftovers that linger in your fridge for a while or you get out your calculator and start dividing a recipe. Well, there's no more of that. *Table for Two* is full of recipes that are perfectly designed for cooking in smaller quantities.

All the recipes are straight-forward and easy to prepare, so you won't feel like you're putting in a huge effort to make a simple meal—but a simple recipe shouldn't cheat you on flavour! Everything's made for maximum flavour impact to satisfy both experienced and novice cooks. To make cooking even easier, we've included tips for purchasing ingredients and hints for turning those unwanted leftovers into time-saving, budget-stretching bonuses.

You'll find all your favourites—including a few you thought couldn't be made in smaller portions, like our Petite Pot Roast, Baby Black Forest Cake and Turkey Shepherd's Pie. We've also created a special small-yield baking section so you'll be able to enjoy muffins,

bread and even biscotti in amounts that won't have your freezer overflowing.

Whether you're a student living on your own, a newlywed or an empty-nester, you're sure to find recipes to suit your every need. A home-cooked meal is always welcome, regardless of your living situation. With straight-forward recipes and a few basic ingredients, you'll have a nutritious, home-cooked meal on the table for you and a dinner companion—without having to worry about what you're going to do with all the leftovers.

Jean Paré

Nutrition Information Guidelines

Each recipe is analyzed using the most current version of the Canadian Nutrient File from Health Canada, which is based on the United States Department of Agriculture (USDA) Nutrient Database.

- If more than one ingredient is listed (such as "butter or hard margarine"), or if a range is given (1 – 2 tsp., 5 – 10 mL), only the first ingredient or first amount is analyzed.

- For meat, poultry and fish, the serving size per person is based on the recommended 4 oz. (113 g) uncooked weight (without bone), which is 2 – 3 oz. (57 – 85 g) cooked weight (without bone)—approximately the size of a deck of playing cards.

- Milk used is 1% M.F. (milk fat), unless otherwise stated.

- Cooking oil used is canola oil, unless otherwise stated.

- Ingredients indicating "sprinkle," "optional," or "for garnish" are not included in the nutrition information.

- The fat in recipes and combination foods can vary greatly depending on the sources and types of fats used in each specific ingredient. For these reasons, the amount of saturated, monounsaturated and polyunsaturated fats may not add up to the total fat content.

Vera C. Mazurak, Ph.D.
Nutritionist

Cooking for two or just for you.

Tips for cooking in smaller portions

If you've ever found a trip to the grocery store to be challenging when you're shopping for a small group, here are a few tips that can help you to keep variety in your pantry, without having to commit to huge quantities.

Shopping for ingredients

There are more and more ingredients available in smaller portions to accommodate couples and even singles who enjoy a home-cooked meal. You'll find that ingredients like pasta sauces and canned foods are available in smaller packages. Of course, if you do happen to purchase ingredients in larger portions, some leftover canned foods like sauces or beans can easily be frozen and used later on.

The produce section sells loose celery stalks, carrots and broccoli florets. Rather than buying a bag of carrots or a whole head of celery, you may find it more economical in the long-run to purchase these items loose. Even though the price may be a little higher on average, if you're not throwing away a whole bunch of food that spoils in your fridge, you may just be saving yourself money!

Meat is often available in smaller portions also. Your butcher may be able to package small portions of ground meats or individual steaks for you. However, if you do have some space in your freezer, you can buy larger quantities of meats and divide them into meal-sized portions yourself. Freezer bags are a convenient option for freezing portions of meat.

Remember, you can often find your dry ingredients in the bulk section. This includes things like chocolate chips, nuts and pasta. If you're only buying what you need and no more, it'll save you from having huge amounts of ingredients pile up in your pantry.

Planning makes perfect

Making a menu plan is a great way to anticipate what you're going to need before you go to the grocery store. If you set aside one night a week to sit down and think about what you might like to eat, you'll find your trips to the grocery store are more productive, and you'll avoid emergency shopping trips to pick up any items you may have forgotten.

You can also anticipate leftovers if you plan in advance and work them into your weekly menu. We like to call these "plan-overs." For example, if you cook a whole chicken one night, you can add the leftover chicken to a salad the following evening. This will help you to avoid throwing food away and help to keep variety in your diet!

Cooking for one

If you're cooking for yourself, some of these recipes can be easily divided in half to make one serving; however, sometimes having leftovers is a good thing! Here are a few options for what you can do with leftovers:

- Lunch the following day
- A convenient dinner that only needs reheating the following night
- Portion the leftovers and freeze for a quick meal on a time-crunched day
- Use leftovers as "plan-overs" and incorporate them into meals later on in the week

Denver Bake

If you think all brunch dishes need to include eggs, this uptown version of mac 'n' cheese will convince you otherwise.

Water	2 cups	500 mL
Salt	1/8 tsp.	0.5 mL
Orzo	1/3 cup	75 mL
Cooking oil	1/2 tsp.	2 mL
Chopped onion	1/3 cup	75 mL
Finely chopped deli ham	1/2 cup	125 mL
Finely chopped red pepper	1/4 cup	60 mL
Grated sharp Cheddar cheese	1/2 cup	125 mL
Ricotta cheese	1/2 cup	125 mL
Fine dry bread crumbs	2 tbsp.	30 mL
Pepper	1/8 tsp.	0.5 mL

Combine water and salt in medium saucepan. Bring to a boil. Add pasta. Boil, uncovered, for about 8 minutes, stirring occasionally, until tender but firm. Drain. Return to same pot. Cover to keep warm.

Heat cooking oil in small frying pan on medium. Add onion. Cook for about 5 minutes, stirring often, until softened.

Add ham and red pepper. Cook for about 3 minutes, stirring occasionally, until red pepper is tender-crisp. Add pasta. Stir.

Combine remaining 4 ingredients in medium bowl. Add pasta mixture. Stir. Spread evenly in greased 2 cup (500 mL) casserole. Bake, uncovered, in 425°F (220°C) oven for about 20 minutes until golden. Serves 2.

1 serving: 469 Calories; 24.4 g Total Fat (6.0 g Mono, 1.2 g Poly, 12.9 g Sat); 86 mg Cholesterol; 31 g Carbohydrate; 2 g Fibre; 30 g Protein; 351 mg Sodium

Pita Steak Sandwiches

Tender beef and refreshing homemade salsa top warm pitas for a unique open-faced sandwich. Greek-style pita breads work best because they're a little sturdier than other varieties, which helps to hold all the filling.

Beef top sirloin steak, trimmed of fat	1/2 lb.	225 g
Salt	1/8 tsp.	0.5 mL
Pepper	1/8 tsp.	0.5 mL
TOMATO CORN SALSA		
Chopped fresh tomato	1/2 cup	125 mL
Frozen kernel corn, thawed	1/4 cup	60 mL
Chopped fresh cilantro or parsley	1 tsp.	5 mL
(or 1/4 tsp., 1 mL, dried)		
Olive (or cooking) oil	1 tsp.	5 mL
Red wine vinegar	1 tsp.	5 mL
Chili powder	1/4 tsp.	1 mL
Ground cumin	1/4 tsp.	1 mL
Salt	1/8 tsp.	0.5 mL
Greek-style pita breads, warmed	2	2

Put steak on greased broiler pan. Sprinkle with salt and pepper. Broil on top rack in oven for about 3 minutes per side or until beef reaches desired doneness. Cover with foil. Let stand for 10 minutes. Cut diagonally, across the grain, into thin slices.

Tomato Corn Salsa: Combine next 8 ingredients in small bowl. Makes about 2/3 cup (150 mL) salsa.

Put pitas on 2 plates. Arrange steak over top. Top with Tomato Corn Salsa. Serves 2.

1 serving: 385 Calories; 11.3 g Total Fat (5.0 g Mono, 1.0 g Poly, 3.6 g Sat); 60 mg Cholesterol; 39 g Carbohydrate; 3 g Fibre; 31 g Protein; 677 mg Sodium

Pictured on page 18.

Irish Breakfast

A complete breakfast—Irish style! You could use pastrami from the deli or leftover corned beef if you have any.

CORNED BEEF HASH

Butter (or hard margarine)	1 tbsp.	15 mL
Finely chopped onion	1/3 cup	75 mL
Finely diced cooked peeled potato	1 1/2 cups	375 mL
Finely chopped deli corned beef (about 3 1/2 oz., 100 g)	3/4 cup	175 mL
Pepper	1/4 tsp.	1 mL
Chopped fresh chives	2 tsp.	10 mL

POACHED EGGS

Water, approximately	4 cups	1 L
White vinegar	2 tsp.	10 mL
Large eggs	4	4
Chopped fresh chives	1 tsp.	5 mL
Pepper, sprinkle		

Corned Beef Hash: Melt butter in medium frying pan on medium. Add onion. Cook for about 3 minutes, stirring occasionally, until onion is starting to brown.

Add potato. Cook for about 5 minutes, stirring occasionally, until potato is golden.

Add corned beef and pepper. Heat and stir for about 1 minute until corned beef is heated through. Add chives. Stir. Makes about 1 1/2 cups (375 mL) Corned Beef Hash. Remove from heat. Cover to keep warm.

Poached Eggs: Pour water into medium saucepan until 1 1/2 inches (3.8 cm) deep. Add vinegar. Stir. Bring to a boil. Reduce heat to medium. Water should continue to simmer. Break 1 egg into shallow dish. Slip egg into water. Repeat with remaining eggs. Cook for 2 to 3 minutes until egg whites are set and yolks reach desired doneness. Transfer eggs with slotted spoon to paper towels to drain. Spoon corned beef mixture onto 2 plates. Top with eggs.

Sprinkle with chives and pepper. Serves 2.

1 serving: 356 Calories; 16.2 g Total Fat (1.5 g Mono, 0.3 g Poly, 7.5 g Sat); 471 mg Cholesterol; 28 g Carbohydrate; 3 g Fibre; 23 g Protein; 803 mg Sodium

Pictured on page 17.

Lemon Poppy Seed Pancakes

A twist of lemon and a sprinkle of poppy seeds provide a delicious addition to this breakfast classic.

All-purpose flour	3/4 cup	175 mL
Granulated sugar	2 tbsp.	30 mL
Baking powder	2 tsp.	10 mL
Poppy seeds	1 1/2 tsp.	7 mL
Salt	1/4 tsp.	1 mL
Large egg, fork-beaten	1	1
Milk	2/3 cup	150 mL
Butter (or hard margarine), melted	1 1/2 tbsp.	25 mL
Grated lemon zest (see Tip, below)	1 tbsp.	15 mL
Lemon juice	1 tbsp.	15 mL

Combine first 5 ingredients in medium bowl. Make a well in centre.

Combine remaining 5 ingredients in small bowl. Add to well. Stir until just moistened. Batter will be lumpy. Preheat griddle to medium-high (see Note). Spray with cooking spray. Pour batter onto griddle, using about 1/2 cup (125 mL) for each pancake. Cook for about 3 minutes until bubbles form on top and edges appear dry. Turn pancakes over. Cook for about 3 minutes until golden. Remove to plate. Makes 4 pancakes. Serves 2.

1 serving: 374 Calories; 12.8 g Total Fat (2.5 g Mono, 0.3 g Poly, 6.8 g Sat); 135 mg Cholesterol; 55 g Carbohydrate; 1 g Fibre; 11 g Protein; 977 mg Sodium

Note: If you don't have an electric griddle, use a large frying pan. Heat 1 tsp. (5 mL) cooking oil on medium. Heat more cooking oil with each batch if necessary to prevent sticking.

tip When a recipe calls for grated lemon zest and juice, it's easier to grate the lemon first, then juice it. Be careful not to grate down to the pith (white part of the peel), which is bitter and best avoided.

Cinnamon Fruit Crepes

The best of both worlds—these decadent crepes are topped with healthy yogurt, granola and fresh fruit. Sure to become a brunch or breakfast favourite. Garnish with a sprinkle of granola and some fresh raspberries for special occasions.

CINNAMON CREPES		
All-purpose flour	1/4 cup	60 mL
Ground cinnamon	1/4 tsp.	1 mL
Salt, just a pinch		
Large egg	1	1
Milk	1/4 cup	60 mL
Butter (or hard margarine), melted	1 tsp.	5 mL
Butter (or hard margarine)	1 tsp.	5 mL
TOPPING		
Fresh raspberries	1/2 cup	125 mL
Sliced banana	1/2 cup	125 mL
Vanilla yogurt	1/2 cup	125 mL
Granola	1/4 cup	60 mL

Cinnamon Crepes: Combine first 3 ingredients in small bowl. Make a well in centre.

Whisk next 3 ingredients in separate small bowl. Add to well. Whisk until smooth. Let stand, covered, for 1 hour. Stir.

Melt 1/4 tsp. (1 mL) of second amount of butter in small (8 inch, 20 cm) non-stick frying pan on medium. Pour about 2 1/2 tbsp. (37 mL) batter into pan. Immediately swirl pan to coat bottom, lifting and tilting pan to ensure entire bottom is covered. Cook until top is set. Turn. Cook until brown spots appear on bottom. Remove to plate. Cover to keep warm. Repeat with remaining butter and crepe batter. Makes about 4 crepes.

Topping: Combine all 4 ingredients in small bowl. Fold crepes into quarters to form triangles. Arrange on 2 plates. Spoon topping over crepes. Serves 2.

1 serving: 249 Calories; 8.5 g Total Fat (1.1 g Mono, 0.2 g Poly, 3.9 g Sat); 123 mg Cholesterol; 35 g Carbohydrate; 2 g Fibre; 10 g Protein; 121 mg Sodium

Pictured on page 17.

Apple Carrot Tuna Melts

The sweetness and crunch of apple and carrot pair with sharp Cheddar cheese for a tuna melt with a totally modern twist. Any variety of apple will work in this recipe, but a Granny Smith is a nice choice for its tartness and crunch.

Can of chunk light tuna in water, drained	6 oz.	170 g
Chopped peeled tart apple	1/4 cup	60 mL
(such as Granny Smith)		
Grated carrot	1/4 cup	60 mL
Mayonnaise	1/4 cup	60 mL
Chopped fresh chives	1 tbsp.	15 mL
(or 3/4 tsp., 4 mL, dried)		
Pepper, just a pinch		
Multi-grain bread slices, toasted	2	2
Grated sharp Cheddar cheese	1/2 cup	125 mL
Chopped fresh chives (optional)	1 tbsp.	15 mL

Combine first 6 ingredients in small bowl.

Arrange toast slices on ungreased baking sheet. Spoon tuna mixture onto toast. Sprinkle with cheese. Broil on top rack in oven for about 2 minutes until cheese is melted.

Sprinkle with second amount of chives. Serves 2.

1 serving: 517 Calories; 35.0 g Total Fat (3.3 g Mono, 1.2 g Poly, 9.6 g Sat); 75 mg Cholesterol; 18 g Carbohydrate; 5 g Fibre; 31 g Protein; 791 mg Sodium

Paré Pointer

If you want to have breakfast in bed every morning, sleep in the kitchen.

Baked Banana Pancake

Not your traditional pancake—this one bakes up light and airy in your oven. Be as creative as you like and try substituting the bananas with other fruit toppings.

All-purpose flour	1/2 cup	125 mL
Granulated sugar	3 tbsp.	50 mL
Baking powder	1 tbsp.	15 mL
Salt	1/4 tsp.	1 mL
Large eggs	2	2
Milk	1/2 cup	125 mL
Butter (or hard margarine), melted	2 tbsp.	30 mL
Maple (or maple-flavoured) syrup	1/4 cup	60 mL
Thinly sliced banana	1 1/3 cups	325 mL

Combine first 4 ingredients in medium bowl. Make a well in centre.

Whisk next 3 ingredients in small bowl. Add to well. Stir until just moistened. Batter will be lumpy. Pour into greased 8 inch (20 cm) round pan. Bake in 400°F (205°C) oven for about 10 minutes until wooden pick inserted in centre of pancake comes out clean. Turn out onto plate.

Drizzle with syrup. Top with banana. Serves 2.

1 serving: 580 Calories; 16.9 g Total Fat (3.3 g Mono, 0.5 g Poly, 9.2 g Sat); 249 mg Cholesterol; 99 g Carbohydrate; 3 g Fibre; 12 g Protein; 1298 mg Sodium

1. "Bee"utiful Fruit Salad, page 23
2. Irish Breakfast, page 12
3. Cinnamon Fruit Crepes, page 14

Props courtesy of: Casa Bugatti
Stokes

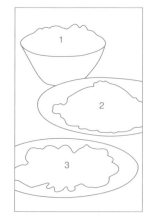

Smoked Salmon BLTs

The BLT sandwich meets lox and bagel. The result? A delicious sandwich bursting with flavour!

Chopped smoked salmon (about 3 oz., 85 g)	1/2 cup	125 mL
Spreadable cream cheese	1/4 cup	60 mL
Finely chopped red onion	1 tbsp.	15 mL
Lemon juice	1 tsp.	5 mL
Chopped capers (optional)	1 tsp.	5 mL
Bacon slices, cooked crisp	4	4
Romaine lettuce leaves	2	2
Small tomato, sliced	1	1
Plain bagels, halved and toasted	2	2

Combine first 5 ingredients in small bowl.

Layer next 3 ingredients, in order given, on bottom halves of bagels. Spoon salmon mixture on top. Cover with top halves of bagels. Makes 2 sandwiches.

1 sandwich: 513 Calories; 19.8 g Total Fat (3.2 g Mono, 1.1 g Poly, 10.2 g Sat); 54 mg Cholesterol; 57 g Carbohydrate; 4 g Fibre; 25 g Protein; 1248 mg Sodium

Pictured at left.

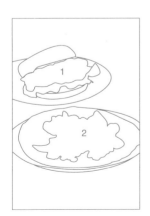

1. Smoked Salmon BLTs, above
2. Pita Steak Sandwiches, page 11

Bacon Artichoke French Toast

This one-dish breakfast is prepared the night before and baked the next morning. Similar to a strata, this unique French toast is great for a leisurely breakfast or brunch.

Cooking oil	1/2 tsp.	2 mL
Sliced fresh white mushrooms	1 cup	250 mL
Chopped back (Canadian) bacon	1/3 cup	75 mL
Italian seasoning	1/2 tsp.	2 mL
Jar of marinated artichoke hearts, drained and chopped	6 oz.	170 mL
Grated mozzarella cheese	1/4 cup	60 mL
Whole-wheat bread slices	4	4
Large eggs, fork-beaten	2	2
Milk	1/3 cup	75 mL
Salt	1/8 tsp.	0.5 mL
Pepper, sprinkle		
Grated mozzarella cheese	1/2 cup	125 mL
Italian seasoning	1/8 tsp.	0.5 mL

Heat cooking oil in medium frying pan on medium. Add next 3 ingredients. Cook for about 5 minutes until mushrooms are softened.

Add artichoke. Heat and stir for 1 minute. Remove from heat. Let stand for about 5 minutes until cooled.

Add first amount of cheese. Stir.

Line bottom of greased glass 9 x 5 x 3 inch (22 x 12.5 x 7.5 cm) loaf pan with 2 bread slices, trimming to fit. Spread mushroom mixture over bread. Cover with remaining bread slices, trimming to fit.

Whisk next 4 ingredients in small bowl until smooth. Pour over bread. Let stand, covered, in refrigerator for at least 6 hours or overnight.

Combine second amount of cheese with second amount of Italian seasoning in small bowl. Sprinkle over bread. Bake in 350°F (175°C) oven for 30 to 35 minutes until edges are golden and knife inserted in centre comes out clean. Let stand for 10 minutes. Serves 2.

1 serving: 321 Calories; 11.3 g Total Fat (2.1 g Mono, 0.8 g Poly, 4.1 g Sat); 237 mg Cholesterol; 25 g Carbohydrate; 2 g Fibre; 30 g Protein; 1274 mg Sodium

Sweet Corn And Scallop Frittata

This frittata is sweet all around—scallops have a natural sweetness that goes great with sweet corn. A nice, light lunch or dinner when served with a crisp green salad.

Butter (or hard margarine)	1 tbsp.	15 mL
Frozen kernel corn	1 cup	250 mL
Chopped onion	1/4 cup	60 mL
Large eggs, fork-beaten	3	3
Grated havarti cheese	1/2 cup	125 mL
Chopped small bay scallops	1/3 cup	75 mL
Milk	2 tbsp.	30 mL
Chopped fresh thyme	1 tsp.	5 mL
Salt	1/4 tsp.	1 mL
Pepper	1/4 tsp.	1 mL

Melt butter in medium frying pan on medium. Add corn and onion. Cook for about 3 minutes, stirring often, until onion is starting to soften.

Combine remaining 7 ingredients in medium bowl. Pour over corn mixture. Heat and stir for 30 seconds. Spread evenly. Reduce heat to medium-low. Cook, covered, for about 5 minutes until bottom is golden and top is almost set. Broil on centre rack in oven (see Tip, below) for about 3 minutes until frittata is set. Serves 2.

1 serving: 516 Calories; 34.5 g Total Fat (4.8 g Mono, 1.4 g Poly, 20.4 g Sat); 359 mg Cholesterol; 17 g Carbohydrate; 2 g Fibre; 28 g Protein; 806 mg Sodium

 tip   When baking or broiling food in a frying pan with a handle that isn't ovenproof, wrap the handle in foil and keep it to the front of the oven, away from the element.

Strawberry Rhubarb Oats

Enjoy the flavours of your favourite pie in a hearty oatmeal. Dress it up with a dollop of vanilla yogurt and some sliced fresh strawberries.

Water	2 cups	500 mL
Large flake rolled oats	1 cup	250 mL
Chopped fresh (or frozen) rhubarb	1/2 cup	125 mL
Chopped fresh (or frozen) strawberries	1/2 cup	125 mL
Brown sugar, packed	1/4 cup	60 mL
Ground cinnamon	1/4 tsp.	1 mL
Salt	1/4 tsp.	1 mL
Ground nutmeg, just a pinch		

Combine all 8 ingredients in medium saucepan. Bring to a boil. Reduce heat to medium-low. Cook, partially covered, for about 15 minutes, stirring occasionally, until oats are tender and mixture has thickened. Makes about 2 2/3 cups (650 mL). Serves 2.

1 serving: 285 Calories; 2.7 g Total Fat (trace Mono, 0.1 g Poly, trace Sat); 0 mg Cholesterol; 59 g Carbohydrate; 5 g Fibre; 8 g Protein; 303 mg Sodium

Avocado Shrimp Cocktails

Light and summery luncheon fare. Avocado pairs perfectly with cilantro and mildly spicy shrimp.

Cooked baby shrimp (about 1 cup, 250 mL)	5 oz.	140 g
Mayonnaise	2 tbsp.	30 mL
Chopped fresh cilantro or parsley	2 tsp.	10 mL
Lime juice	1 tsp.	5 mL
Sweet chili sauce	1 tsp.	5 mL
Salt, just a pinch		
Small avocado	1	1

Fresh cilantro or parsley leaves, for garnish
Lime wedges, for garnish

(continued on next page)

Combine first 6 ingredients in small bowl.

Cut avocado into 12 wedges. Arrange on 2 salad plates. Spoon shrimp mixture alongside.

Garnish with cilantro leaves and lime wedges. Serve immediately. Serves 2.

1 serving: 355 Calories; 26 g Total Fat (9.9 g Mono, 1.8 g Poly, 3.6 g Sat); 235 mg Cholesterol; 10 g Carbohydrate; 7 g Fibre; 22 g Protein; 1403 mg Sodium

"Bee"utiful Fruit Salad

This fruit salad is the bee's knees. Fresh mint and cinnamon honey accent sweet, fresh fruit. Great for a light breakfast or as a part of your next brunch menu.

Ground cinnamon	1/4 tsp.	1 mL
Liquid honey	1 tbsp.	15 mL
Cubed cantaloupe	1/2 cup	125 mL
Cubed fresh pineapple	1/2 cup	125 mL
Cubed ripe mango	1/2 cup	125 mL
Seedless green grapes	1/2 cup	125 mL
Sliced fresh strawberries	1/2 cup	125 mL
Chopped fresh mint	1 tbsp.	15 mL

Combine cinnamon and honey in medium bowl.

Add remaining 6 ingredients. Toss gently until coated. Makes about 2 cups (500 mL). Serves 2.

1 serving: 135 Calories; 0.4 g Total Fat (0.1 g Mono, 0.2 g Poly, 0.1 g Sat); 0 mg Cholesterol; 34 g Carbohydrate; 3 g Fibre; 1 g Protein; 9 mg Sodium

Pictured on page 17.

Prosciutto-Wrapped Chicken

This delicious Asian-flavoured chicken roll can be served as a finger food or over a bed of lettuce for a unique salad—now that's versatility!

Soy sauce	2 tsp.	10 mL
Garlic clove, minced	1	1
(or 1/4 tsp., 1 mL, powder)		
Ground ginger	1/4 tsp.	1 mL
Sesame oil (for flavour)	1/4 tsp.	1 mL
Thin prosciutto (or deli ham) slices, cut in half	3	3
Boneless, skinless chicken breast half, cut into 6 equal pieces	6 oz.	170 g

Combine first 4 ingredients in small bowl.

Roll prosciutto tightly around chicken. Brush with soy sauce mixture. Let stand, covered, for 10 minutes. Arrange, seam-side down, on greased baking sheet. Bake in 400°F (205°C) oven for about 15 minutes until chicken is no longer pink inside and internal temperature reaches 170°F (77°C). Serves 2.

1 serving: 158 Calories; 5.4 g Total Fat (1.2 g Mono, 0.8 g Poly, 1.5 g Sat); 66 mg Cholesterol; 2 g Carbohydrate; trace Fibre; 25 g Protein; 869 mg Sodium

Pictured on page 126.

Granola Chewies

This sweet snack is sure to please, no matter the age of your dinner companion! The addition of granola and sunflower seeds makes this a nutritious grown-up snack, but kids will still love it.

Large marshmallows (see Note)	16	16
Butter (or hard margarine)	1 tbsp.	15 mL
White corn syrup	1 tbsp.	15 mL
Granola with raisins	1 cup	250 mL
Crisp rice cereal	1/3 cup	75 mL
Unsalted, roasted sunflower seeds	2 tbsp.	30 mL

(continued on next page)

24 Snacks & Starters

Combine first 3 ingredients in small saucepan. Heat and stir on medium for about 5 minutes until marshmallows are almost melted. Remove from heat. Stir until smooth.

Add remaining 3 ingredients. Stir. Press evenly in greased 6 inch (15 cm) foil pie plate. Let stand until cool. Cuts into 4 wedges.

1 wedge: 293 Calories; 9.9 g Total Fat (1.1 g Mono, 1.4 g Poly, 2.0 g Sat); 8 mg Cholesterol; 50 g Carbohydrate; trace Fibre; 4 g Protein; 72 mg Sodium

Note: You can use 1 1/2 cups (375 mL) miniature marshmallows instead of large marshmallows.

Red Pepper Feta Dip With Chips

Creamy dip with a hint of smokiness from roasted red peppers. Don't worry about having leftovers—it also works great as a tasty sandwich spread.

DIP

Crumbled feta cheese	3/4 cup	175 mL
Roasted red peppers, drained	1/2 cup	125 mL
Granulated sugar	1 tsp.	5 mL
Red wine vinegar	1 tsp.	5 mL
Garlic powder	1/8 tsp.	0.5 mL
Paprika	1/8 tsp.	0.5 mL
Pepper, just a pinch		

PITA CHIPS

Pita breads (7 inch, 18 cm, diameter)	2	2
Olive (or cooking) oil	1 tbsp.	15 mL
Paprika, sprinkle		
Salt, sprinkle		

Dip: Process all 7 ingredients in blender or food processor until smooth. Makes about 1 cup (250 mL).

Pita Chips: Brush pitas with olive oil. Cut into 8 wedges each. Sprinkle with paprika and salt. Arrange in single layer on ungreased baking sheet. Bake in 375°F (190°C) oven for 5 minutes. Turn. Bake for about 2 minutes until golden. Makes 16 chips. Serve with dip. Serves 2.

1 serving: 458 Calories; 19.9 g Total Fat (7.7 g Mono, 1.2 g Poly, 9.7 g Sat); 52 mg Cholesterol; 48 g Carbohydrate; 1 g Fibre; 16 g Protein; 1546 mg Sodium

Layered Fiesta Dip

Let the fiesta begin! Serve with crackers or tortilla chips. This dip can be prepared a few hours in advance and chilled until you're ready to serve it.

Vegetable (or plain) cream cheese	1/3 cup	75 mL
Chunky hot salsa	3 tbsp.	50 mL
Cooked salad shrimp	2 1/2 oz.	70 g
(about 1/2 cup, 125 mL)		
Chopped tomato	1/4 cup	60 mL
Chopped avocado	1/4 cup	60 mL
Chopped yellow (or red) pepper	2 tbsp.	30 mL

Layer all 6 ingredients, in order given, on small plate. Makes about 1 1/2 cups (375 mL). Serves 2.

1 serving: 257 Calories; 21.7 g Total Fat (3.0 g Mono, 2.5 g Poly, 10.4 g Sat); 91 mg Cholesterol; 7 g Carbohydrate; 2 g Fibre; 9 g Protein; 454 mg Sodium

Pictured on page 126.

Creamy Tapenade Spread

This creamy take on tapenade makes the perfect spread for crackers, crostini or toast points. You can also use it as a dip for veggie sticks.

Black olive tapenade	1/3 cup	75 mL
Ricotta cheese	1/4 cup	60 mL
Chopped fresh parsley	2 tsp.	10 mL
(or 1/2 tsp., 2 mL, flakes)		
Olive oil	2 tsp.	10 mL
Coarsely ground pepper	1/4 tsp.	1 mL

Combine all 5 ingredients in small bowl. Makes about 2/3 cup (150 mL). Serves 2.

1 serving: 178 Calories; 10.6 g Total Fat (3.3 g Mono, 0.4 g Poly, 2.0 g Sat); 10 mg Cholesterol; 15 g Carbohydrate; 1 g Fibre; 5 g Protein; 301 mg Sodium

Warm Shrimp Bruschetta

A new twist on bruschetta with the addition of tender shrimp and bold oregano. Serve as an appetizer or pair with a hearty soup or salad for lunch.

Olive (or cooking) oil	1/2 tsp.	2 mL
Uncooked shrimp (peeled and deveined), chopped	2 oz.	57 g
Small garlic clove, minced (or 1/8 tsp., 0.5 mL, powder)	1	1
Diced tomato	1/4 cup	60 mL
Dried oregano	1/8 tsp.	0.5 mL
Salt, just a pinch		
Pepper, just a pinch		
Chopped fresh basil (or 1/2 tsp., 2 mL, dried)	2 tsp.	10 mL
Lemon juice	1/2 tsp.	2 mL
Baguette bread slices (1/4 inch, 6 mm, thick), toasted	6	6

Heat olive oil in small frying pan on medium-high. Add shrimp and garlic. Stir-fry for about 1 minute until shrimp start to turn pink.

Add next 4 ingredients. Stir-fry for about 1 minute until tomato is heated through. Remove from heat.

Add basil and lemon juice. Stir.

Spoon onto toast slices. Serves 2.

1 serving: 87 Calories; 2.1 g Total Fat (1 g Mono, 0.3 Poly, 0.3 g Sat); 44 mg Cholesterol; 10 g Carbohydrate; 1 g Fibre; 8 g Protein; 130 mg Sodium

Pictured on page 126.

Chèvre-Stuffed Mushrooms

Stuffed mushrooms have long been popular appetizer fare. This unique version is both sweet and savoury and makes just enough for a quick nibble before dinner is served.

Soft goat (chèvre) cheese, cut up	3 tbsp.	50 mL
Chopped dried cranberries	2 tbsp.	30 mL
Chopped pecans, toasted	1 tbsp.	15 mL
(see Tip, page 103)		
Pepper	1/8 tsp.	0.5 mL
Fresh whole white mushrooms	6	6
(2 inch, 5 cm diameter), stems removed		

Combine first 4 ingredients in small bowl.

Spoon into mushrooms. Arrange on greased pie plate. Bake in 400°F (205°C) oven for about 15 minutes until filling starts to brown. Let stand for 1 minute. Serves 2.

1 serving: 101 Calories; 5.8 g Total Fat (2.2 g Mono, 1.0 g Poly, 2.3 g Sat); 6 mg Cholesterol; 9 g Carbohydrate; 1 g Fibre; 5 g Protein; 55 mg Sodium

Pictured on page 126.

Cheese Appies

These crisp little cheese-flavoured crackers make a great partner for tart apple slices. The mixture may appear a bit crumbly at first, but mixing with your hands helps the dough to come together perfectly.

Grated sharp Cheddar cheese	1 cup	250 mL
All-purpose flour	6 tbsp.	100 mL
Cayenne pepper	1/8 tsp.	0.5 mL
Salt	1/8 tsp.	0.5 mL
Cooking oil	1 1/2 tbsp.	25 mL
Unpeeled thin apple slices	12	12

(continued on next page)

Snacks & Starters

Combine first 4 ingredients in medium bowl.

Add cooking oil. Mix with hands until moistened. Pat into log, about 1 1/2 inch (3.8 cm) in diameter. Wrap in waxed paper. Chill for about 2 hours until firm. Discard waxed paper. Cut into 12 slices with sharp knife. Arrange on greased baking sheet. Bake in 350°F (175°C) oven for about 12 minutes until edges are golden. Transfer crackers immediately to wire rack to cool.

Arrange apple slices over crackers. Makes 12 appies. Serves 2.

1 serving: 411 Calories; 29.0 g Total Fat (11.3 g Mono, 3.6 g Poly, 12.7 g Sat); 59 mg Cholesterol; 22 g Carbohydrate; 1 g Fibre; 16 g Protein; 497 mg Sodium

Apple Colby Bites

Maybe it's the unique range of flavours that makes these bites so special. Or maybe it's the contrasting textures. Regardless, these crisp little toasts are sure to satisfy.

Lemon juice	3/4 tsp.	4 mL
Grated peeled cooking apple	1/4 cup	60 mL
(such as McIntosh)		
Grated colby cheese	1/3 cup	75 mL
Finely diced celery	2 tbsp.	30 mL
Chopped walnuts	1 tbsp.	15 mL
Mayonnaise	1 tbsp.	15 mL
Brown sugar, packed	1/2 tsp.	2 mL
Ground cinnamon	1/8 tsp.	0.5 mL
Curry powder	1/8 tsp.	0.5 mL
Salt, sprinkle		
Baguette bread slices	6	6
(1/2 inch, 12 mm, thick), toasted		

Drizzle lemon juice over apple in small bowl. Toss until coated.

Add next 8 ingredients. Stir well.

Spoon onto toast. Arrange toasts in single layer in small shallow pan. Bake in 350°F (175°C) oven for about 8 minutes until cheese is melted. Serves 2.

1 serving: 264 Calories; 18.8 g Total Fat (2.3 g Mono, 3.0 g Poly, 8.7 g Sat); 44 mg Cholesterol; 14 g Carbohydrate; 1 g Fibre; 12 g Protein; 386 mg Sodium

Lemon Pepper Bread Salad

Bread salads, also known as panzanella, *are becoming very popular. Rustic and hearty salads make great meals—this is one trend you won't want to miss out on!*

Lemon juice	1 tbsp.	15 mL
Olive (or cooking) oil	1 tbsp.	15 mL
Liquid honey	2 tsp.	10 mL
Dijon mustard	1/2 tsp.	2 mL
Fresh spinach leaves, lightly packed	1 cup	250 mL
Grape tomatoes, cut in half	6	6
Butter (or hard margarine)	2 tsp.	10 mL
Olive (or cooking) oil	2 tsp.	10 mL
Whole-wheat bread, cubed	1 cup	250 mL
(about 1/2 inch, 12 mm, pieces)		
Grated lemon zest	1 tsp.	5 mL
Coarsely ground pepper	1/2 tsp.	2 mL
Chopped fresh basil	2 tsp.	10 mL

Whisk first 4 ingredients in medium bowl. Add spinach and tomato. Toss until coated.

Heat butter and olive oil in medium frying pan on medium. Add bread cubes. Cook for about 3 minutes, stirring often, until browned and crisp. Sprinkle with lemon zest and pepper. Toss. Add to spinach mixture.

Sprinkle with basil. Toss. Makes about 2 1/2 cups (625 mL). Serves 2.

1 serving: 225 Calories; 16.1 g Total Fat (9.7 g Mono, 1.4 g Poly, 4.2 g Sat); 10 mg Cholesterol; 19 g Carbohydrate; 3 g Fibre; 3 g Protein; 170 mg Sodium

Pictured on page 35.

Dill Shrimp Penne Salad

All your favourite flavours—together in one refreshing salad.

Water	6 cups	1.5 L
Salt	3/4 tsp.	4 mL
Penne pasta	1 cup	250 mL
Cooked salad shrimp (about 3/4 cup, 175 mL)	6 oz.	170 g
Sliced English cucumber (with peel), about 1/4 inch (6 mm) thick, quartered	1/2 cup	125 mL
Mayonnaise	1/4 cup	60 mL
Chopped fresh dill (or 3/4 tsp., 4 mL, dried)	1 tbsp.	15 mL
Grated lemon zest	1/2 tsp.	2 mL
Pepper	1/4 tsp.	1 mL
Capers (optional)	1 tbsp.	15 mL

Combine water and salt in large saucepan. Bring to a boil. Add pasta. Boil, uncovered, for 14 to 16 minutes, stirring occasionally, until tender but firm. Drain. Rinse with cold water. Drain. Transfer to medium bowl.

Add shrimp and cucumber. Toss.

Combine next 5 ingredients in small bowl. Add to shrimp mixture. Stir until coated. Makes about 3 cups (750 mL). Serves 2.

1 cup (250 mL): 477 Calories; 23.0 g Total Fat (10.1 g Mono, 8.8 g Poly, 2.5 g Sat); 104 mg Cholesterol; 47 g Carbohydrate; 2 g Fibre; 20 g Protein; 370 mg Sodium

Pictured on page 35.

Paré Pointer

The easiest way to increase the size of your paycheck?
Use a magnifying glass.

Festive Cranberry Salad

Whether it's the festive season or not, this sweet salad makes for a colourful addition to your dinner table. Works great for a brunch or lunch.

Water	1/4 cup	60 mL
Reserved juice from fruit cup	3 tbsp.	50 mL
Cranberry jelly powder (gelatin), see Note	1 1/2 tbsp.	25 mL
Cream cheese, cut up	2 tbsp.	30 mL
Fruit cup, drained and juice reserved	4 oz.	107 mL

Combine water and juice in small microwave-safe bowl. Microwave, uncovered, on high (100%) for about 2 minutes until boiling.

Add jelly powder. Stir until dissolved. Add cream cheese. Whisk until smooth. Chill for about 45 minutes until almost set.

Add fruit. Stir. Pour into greased 1 cup (250 mL) mold. Refrigerate for about 2 hours until firm. Loosen salad in mold. Invert onto dampened serving dish. Serves 2.

1 serving: 123 Calories; 4.9 g Total Fat (1.4 g Mono, 0.2 g Poly, 3.1 g Sat); 16 mg Cholesterol; 18 g Carbohydrate; trace Fibre; 2 g Protein; 82 mg Sodium

Note: You can buy jelly powder in some bulk stores, but if you're using jelly powder from a box, this recipe calls for 1/4 of a 3 oz. (85 g) box. You could use these proportions to make this salad 4 times or combine the remaining powder with 3/4 of the liquid recommended in the instructions on the box.

 tip To julienne, cut into very thin strips that resemble matchsticks.

Asian Egg Thread Soup

Tangy and with just enough heat, this colourful soup is so simple to make.
For the most visually appealing soup, choose a stir-fry mix that includes baby
corn, water chestnuts, carrots and snow peas.

Sesame (or cooking) oil	1/2 tsp.	2 mL
Sliced fresh brown (or white) mushrooms	1/2 cup	125 mL
Prepared chicken broth	2 cups	500 mL
Frozen mixed stir-fry vegetables, larger pieces chopped	1/2 cup	125 mL
Sliced deli roast pork, julienned (see Tip, page 32), about 1/3 cup (75 mL)	1 3/4 oz.	50
Soy sauce	1 tbsp.	15 mL
Sweet chili sauce	1 tbsp.	15 mL
White vinegar	1 tbsp.	15 mL
Dry sherry (or water)	1 tbsp.	15 mL
Cornstarch	1 tbsp.	15 mL
Large egg	1	1
Sliced green onion	1 tbsp.	15 mL

Heat sesame oil in medium saucepan on medium-high. Add mushrooms.
Cook for about 5 minutes, stirring occasionally, until mushrooms are
softened and starting to brown.

Add next 6 ingredients. Cook for about 5 minutes, stirring occasionally,
until boiling and vegetables are tender-crisp.

Stir sherry into cornstarch in small cup. Stir into soup. Heat and stir until
boiling and thickened.

Beat egg with fork in small cup. Add to soup in thin, steady stream, stirring
constantly, until fine threads form.

Sprinkle with green onion. Makes about 2 1/2 cups (625 mL). Serves 2.

1 serving: 162 Calories; 6.4 g Total Fat (1.9 g Mono, 1.2 g Poly, 1.7 g Sat); 111 mg Cholesterol;
13 g Carbohydrate; trace Fibre; 10 g Protein; 2316 mg Sodium

Sunny Citrus Salads

Delicate butter lettuce provides the perfect bed for fresh citrus fruit, crunchy almonds and a light mint dressing. Capture the juice to use in the dressing as you segment the orange.

Cut or torn butter lettuce, lightly packed	4 cups	1 L
Medium pink grapefruit, segmented (see Tip, page 113)	1	1
Medium orange, segmented (see Tip, page 113)	1	1
Sliced natural almonds, toasted (see Tip, page 103)	2 tbsp.	30 mL
Chopped dried figs (optional)	2 tbsp.	30 mL
MINT VINAIGRETTE		
Orange juice	2 tbsp.	30 mL
Cooking oil	1 tbsp.	15 mL
Chopped fresh mint (or 1/2 tsp., 2 mL, dried)	2 tsp.	10 mL
Salt, just a pinch		

Arrange lettuce on 2 plates. Scatter with next 4 ingredients, in order given.

Mint Vinaigrette: Combine all 4 ingredients in small cup. Makes about 3 tbsp. (50 mL) vinaigrette. Drizzle over salads. Serves 2.

1 serving: 228 Calories; 11.6 g Total Fat (6.9 g Mono, 3.2 g Poly, 0.9 g Sat); 0 mg Cholesterol; 32 g Carbohydrate; 12 g Fibre; 5 g Protein; 8 mg Sodium

Pictured on front cover.

1. Lemon Pepper Bread Salad, page 30
2. Dill Shrimp Penne Salad, page 31
3. Barley Apple Salad, page 39

Gingery Noodle Soup

Reminiscent of the clean, fresh flavours of Vietnamese cuisine, this chicken soup is so easy to make at home—it's less trouble than take-out! You can add more chili sauce and herbs according to your preference.

Prepared chicken broth	3 cups	750 mL
Piece of ginger root	1	1
(1 inch, 2.5 cm., length)		
Fish sauce	1 tsp.	5 mL
Sweet chili sauce	1 tsp.	5 mL
Fresh bean sprouts	1/2 cup	125 mL
Shredded cooked chicken	1/2 cup	125 mL
Coarsely chopped fresh cilantro or parsley	1 tbsp.	15 mL
Lime juice	1/2 tsp.	2 mL
Thin rice stick noodles	2 oz.	57 g

Combine first 4 ingredients in medium saucepan. Bring to a boil. Reduce heat to medium-low. Simmer for about 5 minutes until ginger is fragrant. Remove and discard ginger. Remove from heat.

Add next 4 ingredients. Stir. Let stand, covered, for about 5 minutes until heated through.

Put noodles into medium bowl. Cover with boiling water. Let stand for about 3 minutes until tender. Drain. Transfer to 2 large soup bowls. Ladle soup over noodles. Stir. Makes about 3 1/2 cups (875 mL). Serves 2.

1 serving: 272 Calories; 6.2 g Total Fat (2.2 g Mono, 1.6 g Poly, 1.6 g Sat); 51 mg Cholesterol; 31 g Carbohydrate; 1 g Fibre; 22 g Protein; 2581 mg Sodium

Pictured at left.

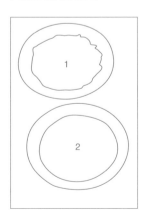

1. Gingery Noodle Soup, above
2. Roasted Red Pepper Soup, page 41

Props courtesy of: Danesco Inc.

French Vegetable Soup

The traditional method of caramelizing vegetables brings out their natural sweetness, and a touch of sherry adds a French twist to this light soup.

Olive (or cooking) oil	1 tsp.	5 mL
Thinly sliced leek (white part only)	1 cup	250 mL
Thinly sliced onion	1 cup	250 mL
Sliced fresh white mushrooms	1 cup	250 mL
Grated carrot	1/2 cup	125 mL
Dried thyme	1/4 tsp.	1 mL
Pepper	1/4 tsp.	1 mL
Granulated sugar	1/2 tsp.	2 mL
Prepared vegetable broth	2 cups	500 mL
Dry sherry	1 tbsp.	15 mL

Heat olive oil in medium saucepan on medium. Add leek and onion. Cook for about 8 minutes, stirring often, until golden.

Add next 4 ingredients. Cook for about 6 minutes, stirring occasionally, until mushrooms are starting to brown and liquid is evaporated.

Add sugar. Heat and stir for 1 minute.

Add broth and sherry. Bring to a boil. Reduce heat to medium. Boil gently, uncovered, for 5 minutes to blend flavours. Makes about 2 cups (500 mL). Serves 2.

1 serving: 144 Calories; 3.1 g Total Fat (1.7 g Mono, 0.4 g Poly, 0.4 g Sat); 0 mg Cholesterol; 26 g Carbohydrate; 4 g Fibre; 3 g Protein; 495 mg Sodium

Paré Pointer

Ali Baba always orders his burgers on an open-sesame bun.

Soups & Salads

Barley Apple Salad

Barley is a filling grain that ought to be a staple. Apple gives a delightful texture to this hearty and nutritious salad.

Prepared vegetable broth	1 1/2 cups	375 mL
Ground cumin	1/8 tsp.	0.5 mL
Pepper	1/8 tsp.	0.5 mL
Pot barley	1/3 cup	75 mL
Diced unpeeled cooking apple (such as McIntosh)	1/2 cup	125 mL
Fresh spinach leaves, lightly packed	1/2 cup	125 mL
Chopped celery	1/4 cup	60 mL
APPLE HONEY DRESSING		
Apple cider vinegar	1 tbsp.	15 mL
Liquid honey	2 tsp.	10 mL
Olive (or cooking) oil	1 tsp.	5 mL
Salt, just a pinch		

Combine first 3 ingredients in small saucepan. Bring to a boil. Add barley. Stir. Reduce heat to medium-low. Simmer, covered, for about 55 minutes, without stirring, until liquid is absorbed and barley is tender. Transfer to medium bowl. Cool.

Add remaining 3 ingredients. Toss.

Apple Honey Dressing: Combine all 4 ingredients in small cup. Makes about 2 tbsp. (30 mL) dressing. Drizzle over barley mixture. Toss until coated. Makes about 2 1/2 cups (625 mL) salad. Serves 2.

1 serving: 205 Calories; 3.2 g Total Fat (1.7 g Mono, 0.4 g Poly, 0.4 g Sat); 0 mg Cholesterol; 41 g Carbohydrate; 5 g Fibre; 4 g Protein; 367 mg Sodium

Pictured on page 35.

Bacon Corn Chipotle Soup

What could be better than the flavours of smoky bacon, chipotle heat and sweet corn? A comforting soup that combines all three!

Bacon slices, chopped	2	2
Chopped onion	1/2 cup	125 mL
Finely chopped celery	1/2 cup	125 mL
Finely chopped chipotle pepper in adobo sauce (see Tip, below)	1/2 tsp.	2 mL
Frozen kernel corn	2 cups	500 mL
Prepared chicken broth	2 cups	500 mL
Salt	1/4 tsp.	1 mL
Half-and-half cream	1/4 cup	60 mL

Cook bacon in medium saucepan on medium until crisp. Remove with slotted spoon to paper-towel lined plate to drain. Drain all but 1/2 tsp. (2 mL) drippings.

Add onion and celery to same saucepan. Cook for about 5 minutes, stirring often, until celery is softened.

Add chipotle pepper. Heat and stir for 1 minute.

Add next 3 ingredients. Stir. Bring to a boil. Reduce heat to medium. Boil gently, uncovered, for about 5 minutes until corn is tender. Remove from heat. Transfer 1 cup (250 mL) corn mixture to small bowl. Set aside. Carefully process remaining soup with hand blender or in blender until smooth (see Safety Tip). Add reserved corn mixture.

Add cream and bacon. Cook and stir until heated through. Makes about 3 1/4 cups (800 mL). Serves 2.

1 serving: 249 Calories; 9.3 g Total Fat (3.1 g Mono, 1.0 g Poly, 3.8 g Sat); 20 mg Cholesterol; 33 g Carbohydrate; 4 g Fibre; 8 g Protein; 1974 mg Sodium

Safety Tip: Follow blender manufacturer's instructions for processing hot liquids.

 Chipotle chili peppers are smoked jalapeño peppers. Be sure to wash your hands after handling. To store any leftover chipotle chili peppers, divide into recipe-friendly portions and freeze, with sauce, in airtight containers for up to one year.

Roasted Red Pepper Soup

Using roasted red peppers from a jar makes this soup quick and easy to prepare, and it's just as delicious as if you'd roasted the peppers yourself.

Butter (or hard margarine)	1 tsp.	5 mL
Chopped onion	1 cup	250 mL
Garlic clove, minced	1	1
(or 1/4 tsp., 1 mL, powder)		
Jar of roasted red peppers, drained	13 oz.	370 mL
Prepared vegetable broth	1 cup	250 mL
Salt	1/8 tsp.	0.5 mL
Half-and-half cream	1/2 cup	125 mL
Chopped fresh basil	1 tbsp.	15 mL
Crumbled blue cheese (optional)	1/4 cup	60 mL

Melt butter in small saucepan on medium. Add onion and garlic. Cook for about 5 minutes, stirring often, until onion is softened.

Add next 3 ingredients. Bring to a boil. Reduce heat to medium-low. Simmer, partially covered, for 15 minutes to blend flavours. Carefully process with hand blender or in blender until smooth (see Safety Tip).

Add cream and basil. Cook and stir until heated through. Makes about 2 1/2 cups (625 mL).

Sprinkle blue cheese over individual servings. Serves 2.

1 serving: 247 Calories; 11.7 g Total Fat (2.6 g Mono, 0.4 g Poly, 5.7 g Sat); 29 mg Cholesterol; 29 g Carbohydrate; 8 g Fibre; 5 g Protein; 1110 mg Sodium

Pictured on page 36.

Safety Tip: Follow blender manufacturer's instructions for processing hot liquids.

Quick Sloppy Joe Pizza

Who needs a bun? Bake your sloppy joe mixture into a pizza crust for a unique spin on this traditional favourite.

Cooking oil	1/2 tsp.	2 mL
Lean ground beef	1/2 lb.	225 g
Chopped fresh white mushrooms	1 cup	250 mL
Chopped onion	1/2 cup	125 mL
Salt	1/8 tsp.	0.5 mL
Pepper	1/4 tsp.	1 mL
Can of pizza sauce	7 1/2 oz.	213 mL
Biscuit mix	1 1/2 cups	375 mL
Boiling water	1/3 cup	75 mL
Biscuit mix	1 tbsp.	15 mL
Grated Italian cheese blend	1/2 cup	125 mL
Diced red pepper	1/4 cup	60 mL

Heat cooking oil in medium frying pan on medium-high. Add next 5 ingredients. Scramble-fry for about 5 minutes until mushrooms are starting to brown and liquid has evaporated.

Add pizza sauce. Stir. Remove from heat.

Stir first amount of biscuit mix and boiling water in medium bowl until soft dough forms. Turn out onto work surface sprinkled with second amount of biscuit mix. Knead 5 or 6 times until smooth. Roll out to 12 inch (30 cm) diameter circle. Transfer to greased baking sheet. Spread beef mixture evenly over dough, leaving a 3 inch (7.5 cm) border.

Sprinkle with cheese and red pepper. Fold a section of border up and over filling. Repeat with next section, allowing pastry to overlap so that fold is created. Pinch fold to seal. Repeat until pastry border is completely folded around filling. Bake in 375°F (190°C) oven for about 25 minutes until crust is golden and cheese is melted. Serves 2.

1 serving: 736 Calories; 29.4 g Total Fat (4.4 g Mono, 0.7 g Poly, 10.2 g Sat); 93 mg Cholesterol; 77 g Carbohydrate; 4 g Fibre; 41 g Protein; 1781 mg Sodium

Pineapple Beef Stir-Fry

Rice is the perfect companion for the sweet and tangy sauce in this super-speedy stir-fry.

Ketchup	2 tbsp.	30 mL
Soy sauce	2 tbsp.	30 mL
Granulated sugar	1 tbsp.	15 mL
Ground ginger	1/4 tsp.	1 mL
Garlic powder	1/8 tsp.	0.5 mL
Beef stir-fry strips	1/2 lb.	225 g
Cooking oil	1 tsp.	5 mL
Cooking oil	1 tsp.	5 mL
Fresh mixed stir-fry vegetables	2 cups	500 mL
Pineapple tidbits, drained and juice reserved	1/2 cup	125 mL
Reserved pineapple juice	1 tbsp.	15 mL
Sesame seeds, toasted (see Tip, page 103)	1 tbsp.	15 mL

Combine first 5 ingredients in small shallow bowl. Reserve 2 tbsp. (30 mL) in small cup. Add beef to bowl. Stir until coated. Let stand, covered, in refrigerator for about 30 minutes. Drain.

Heat medium frying pan or wok on medium-high until very hot. Add first amount of cooking oil. Add beef mixture. Stir-fry for about 2 minutes until beef reaches desired doneness. Transfer to small bowl. Cover to keep warm. Reduce heat to medium.

Add second amount of cooking oil to same frying pan. Add next 3 ingredients. Stir-fry for about 3 minutes until vegetables are tender-crisp. Add beef and reserved ketchup mixture. Heat and stir for about 1 minute until heated through.

Sprinkle with sesame seeds. Makes about 3 cups (750 mL). Serves 2.

1 serving: 346 Calories; 14.8 g Total Fat (6.0 g Mono, 1.7 g Poly, 3.4 g Sat); 60 mg Cholesterol; 26 g Carbohydrate; 3 g Fibre; 28 g Protein; 1140 mg Sodium

Pictured on page 53.

Beef Salad Rolls

Addictively easy and delicious! Find rice paper wrappers in the imported food aisle of your supermarket or at an Asian market.

SPICY DIPPING SAUCE

Rice vinegar	3 tbsp.	50 mL
Granulated sugar	1 tbsp.	15 mL
Sliced green onion	1 tbsp.	15 mL
Sweet chili sauce	1 tbsp.	15 mL
Salt, just a pinch		

ROLLS

Mayonnaise	2 tbsp.	30 mL
Lime juice	1/2 tsp.	2 mL
Sweet chili sauce	1/2 tsp.	2 mL
Curry powder	1/4 tsp.	1 mL
Salt, just a pinch		
Shredded romaine lettuce, lightly packed	1 cup	250 mL
Julienned cooked roast beef (see Tip, page 32)	2/3 cup	150 mL
Finely grated carrot	1/3 cup	75 mL
Julienned English cucumber (with peel), see Tip, page 32	1/3 cup	75 mL
Coarsely chopped fresh cilantro or parsley	2 tbsp.	30 mL
Rice paper rounds (9 inch, 22 cm, diameter)	6	6

Spicy Dipping Sauce: Stir all 5 ingredients in small bowl until sugar is dissolved. Makes about 1/4 cup (60 mL) sauce.

Rolls: Combine first 5 ingredients in medium bowl.

Add next 5 ingredients. Stir until coated.

Place 1 rice paper round in shallow bowl of hot water until just softened. Lay on tea towel. Spread about 6 tbsp. (100 mL) lettuce mixture across centre of wrapper, leaving 1 1/2 inch (3.8 cm) edge on both sides. Fold sides over filling. Roll up tightly from bottom to enclose. Transfer to serving plate. Repeat with remaining wrappers and filling. Makes 6 rolls. Serve with Spicy Dipping Sauce. Serves 2.

1 serving: 364 Calories; 15.7 g Total Fat (1.9 g Mono, 0.3 g Poly, 3.2 g Sat); 62 mg Cholesterol; 33 g Carbohydrate; 1 g Fibre; 24 g Protein; 533 mg Sodium

Beef

Curry Beef And Potato

A mild introduction for those not used to cooking with curry. But, if you're a fan of spicy food, don't be afraid to up the ante—use extra-hot curry paste!

Cooking oil	1 tsp.	5 mL
Lean ground beef	1/2 lb.	225 g
Chopped fresh white mushrooms	1 cup	250 mL
Chopped onion	1/2 cup	125 mL
Curry powder	2 tsp.	10 mL
Soy sauce	2 tsp.	10 mL
Small garlic clove, minced	1	1
(or 1/8 tsp., 0.5 mL, powder)		
Granulated sugar	1/2 tsp.	2 mL
Pepper	1/4 tsp.	1 mL
All-purpose flour	2 tsp.	10 mL
Prepared beef broth	1/3 cup	75 mL
Cubed cooked peeled potato	1/2 cup	125 mL
Frozen peas	1/4 cup	60 mL

Heat cooking oil in medium frying pan on medium-high. Add next 8 ingredients. Scramble-fry for about 7 minutes until beef and mushrooms are browned.

Sprinkle with flour. Heat and stir for 1 minute. Slowly add broth, stirring constantly until smooth. Heat and stir until boiling and thickened.

Add potato and peas. Stir. Reduce heat to medium. Cook, covered, for about 2 minutes until heated through. Makes about 2 1/2 cups (625 mL). Serves 2.

1 serving: 264 Calories; 8.1 g Total Fat (3.6 g Mono, 1.0 g Poly, 2.6 g Sat); 59 mg Cholesterol; 22 g Carbohydrate; 3 g Fibre; 26 g Protein; 842 mg Sodium

Pictured on page 53.

Beef

Petite Pot Roast

Tender roast beef and veggies aren't reserved for larger get-togethers anymore! Cross-rib makes a great pot roast and has a compact shape that lends itself to smaller sizes. You may have to ask the butcher to cut you a roast this size or buy a larger one, cut it and freeze the other half for next time.

Boneless beef cross-rib roast	1 lb.	454 g
Prepared beef broth	2 1/2 cups	625 mL
Baby potatoes, larger ones cut in half	1/2 lb.	225 g
Medium carrots, cut into 1 inch (2.5 cm) pieces	2	2
Small parsnip, cut into 1 inch (2.5 cm) pieces	1	1
Small onion, cut into 4 wedges	1/2	1/2
Minute tapioca	2 tbsp.	30 mL
Tomato paste (see Tip, page 49)	1 tbsp.	15 mL
Soy sauce	1 tsp.	5 mL
Bay leaf	1	1
Garlic clove, minced (or 1/4 tsp., 1 mL, powder)	1	1
Chopped fresh thyme (or 1/8 tsp., 0.5 mL, dried)	1/2 tsp.	2 mL
Salt	1/4 tsp.	1 mL
Pepper	1/8 tsp.	2 mL
Frozen (or fresh) peas	1/2 cup	125 mL

Place roast in greased small roasting pan.

Combine next 13 ingredients in medium bowl. Arrange around roast. Cook, covered, in 350°F (175°C) oven for about 1 1/2 hours until beef is tender. Remove roast to plate. Cover with foil. Let stand for 15 minutes. Cut into 6 slices.

Add peas to vegetable mixture. Stir. Cook, covered, in 350°F (175°C) oven for about 10 minutes until peas are heated through. Discard bay leaf. Serve with beef. Serves 2.

1 serving: 1018 Calories; 64.0 g Total Fat (28 g Mono, 2.4 g Poly, 26.4 g Sat); 148 mg Cholesterol; 65 g Carbohydrate; 10 g Fibre; 44 g Protein; 2462 mg Sodium

Pictured on page 54.

Beef

Blue Cheese Beef Crumble

Forget all those sweet crumbles, this savoury version is sure to be a hit!

Butter (or hard margarine)	1 tsp.	5 mL
Sliced fresh white mushrooms	1 cup	250 mL
Lean ground beef	1/2 lb.	225 g
Half-and-half cream	1/2 cup	125 mL
Chopped fresh rosemary	1 tsp.	5 mL
(or 1/4 tsp., 1 mL, dried, crushed)		
Seasoned salt	1/4 tsp.	1 mL
Pepper	1/4 tsp.	1 mL
All-purpose flour	1/4 cup	60 mL
Baking powder	1/2 tsp.	2 mL
Cold butter (or hard margarine), cut up	2 tbsp.	30 mL
Crumbled blue cheese	2 tbsp.	30 mL
Quick-cooking rolled oats	2 tbsp.	30 mL

Melt butter in medium frying pan on medium-high. Add mushrooms. Cook for about 5 minutes, stirring often, until starting to brown. Transfer to small bowl.

Add beef to same frying pan. Scramble-fry for about 3 minutes until beef is browned.

Add next 4 ingredients and mushrooms. Heat and stir for about 1 minute until boiling. Transfer to 8 x 5 3/8 x 1 3/4 inch (20 x 14 x 3 cm) foil pan.

Combine flour and baking powder in small bowl. Cut in butter until mixture resembles coarse crumbs.

Add cheese and rolled oats. Stir. Sprinkle over beef mixture. Bake in 350°F (175°C) oven for about 30 minutes until topping is crisp and golden. Serves 2.

1 serving: 480 Calories; 32.0 g Total Fat (9.9 g Mono, 1.1 g Poly, 17.8 g Sat); 133 mg Cholesterol; 19 g Carbohydrate; 1 g Fibre; 28 g Protein; 600 mg Sodium

Steak And Mushroom Pies

A timeless pub favourite. With the added decadence of Cheddar cheese in the rich and buttery pastry, you surely won't miss the bottom crust.

CHEDDAR CHEESE PASTRY

All-purpose flour	1/2 cup	125 mL
Salt	1/8 tsp.	0.5 mL
Cold butter	3 tbsp.	50 mL
Finely grated sharp Cheddar cheese	1/4 cup	60 mL
Ice water	1 1/2 tbsp.	25 mL
White vinegar	1/2 tsp.	2 mL

FILLING

Cooking oil	1/2 tsp.	2 mL
Beef rib-eye steak, cut into 3/4 inch (2 cm) cubes	1/2 lb.	225 g
Cooking oil	1/2 tsp.	2 mL
Quartered fresh white mushrooms	1 cup	250 mL
Chopped onion	3/4 cup	175 mL
Dry (or alcohol-free) red wine	2 tbsp.	30 mL
Butter (or hard margarine)	1 tbsp.	15 mL
All-purpose flour	2 tbsp.	30 mL
Chopped fresh thyme (or 1/8 tsp., 0.5 mL, dried)	1/2 tsp.	2 mL
Salt	1/8 tsp.	0.5 mL
Pepper, just a pinch		
Prepared beef broth	1 cup	250 mL
Large egg, fork-beaten	1	1

Cheddar Cheese Pastry: Combine flour and salt in medium bowl. Cut in butter until mixture resembles coarse crumbs. Add cheese. Stir well. Make a well in centre.

Add ice water and vinegar to well, stirring with fork until mixture starts to come together. Do not overmix. Shape into slightly flattened disc. Wrap with plastic wrap. Chill for 1 hour.

(continued on next page)

Beef

Filling: Heat first amount of cooking oil in medium frying pan on medium-high. Add beef. Cook for about 5 minutes, stirring occasionally, until browned. Remove to medium bowl.

Add second amount of cooking oil to same frying pan. Add next 3 ingredients. Cook for about 5 minutes, stirring occasionally, until onion and mushrooms are browned. Add to beef. Reduce heat to medium.

Melt butter in same frying pan. Add next 4 ingredients. Heat and stir for 1 minute. Slowly add broth, stirring constantly with whisk until smooth. Heat and stir until boiling and thickened. Pour over beef mixture. Stir. Makes about 2 cups (500 mL) filling. Spoon into two 5 inch (12.5 cm) foil pot pie plates or 8 oz. (227 mL) ramekins.

Divide pastry in half. Roll out on lightly floured surface to form circles, about 1 inch (2.5 cm) larger than top of dishes. Brush edges of pastry circles with egg. Invert onto pies. Trim and crimp edges to seal. Brush tops with egg. Cut 4 small slits in tops to allow steam to escape. Place on baking sheet. Bake in 375°F (190°C) oven for about 40 minutes until golden brown. Makes 2 pies.

1 pie: 629 Calories; 38.4 g Total Fat (11.1 g Mono, 1.9 g Poly, 20.7 g Sat); 243 mg Cholesterol; 37 g Carbohydrate; 2 g Fibre; 31 g Protein; 1297 mg Sodium

 tip   If a recipe calls for less than an entire can of tomato paste, freeze the unopened can for 30 minutes. Open both ends and push the contents through one end. Slice off only what you need. Freeze the remaining paste in a resealable freezer bag or plastic wrap for future use.

Pizza Aioli Steak Sandwiches

Garlic mayo, also known as aioli, provides the perfect base for a tender steak sandwich that's full of pizza-flavoured veggies. Serve with a salad or fries and you've got dinner!

Mayonnaise	3 tbsp.	50 mL
Garlic clove, minced (or 1/4 tsp., 1 mL, powder)	1	1
Dried crushed chilies	1/8 tsp.	0.5 mL
Cooking oil	1 tsp.	5 mL
Beef top sirloin steak, cut across the grain into 1/8 inch (3 mm) slices (see Tip, page 93)	1/2 lb.	225 g
Seasoned salt	1/2 tsp.	2 mL
Sliced green pepper	1/4 cup	60 mL
Sliced onion	1/4 cup	60 mL
Italian seasoning	1/2 tsp.	2 mL
Canned diced tomatoes, drained	1/2 cup	125 mL
French bread slices (about 1 inch, 2.5 cm, thick), toasted	2	2

Combine first 3 ingredients in small cup. Set aside.

Heat medium frying pan on medium-high until very hot. Add cooking oil. Add beef. Stir-fry for about 4 minutes until beef reaches desired doneness. Sprinkle with seasoned salt. Stir. Transfer to small bowl. Cover to keep warm.

Add next 3 ingredients to same frying pan. Stir-fry for about 3 minutes until vegetables are tender-crisp.

Add tomatoes and beef. Heat and stir for about 1 minute until heated through.

Spread mayonnaise mixture on 1 side of each toast slice. Spoon beef mixture over top. Serves 2.

1 serving: 547 Calories; 28.9 g Total Fat (5.4 g Mono, 1.4 g Poly, 6.0 g Sat); 68 mg Cholesterol; 38 g Carbohydrate; 3 g Fibre; 31 g Protein; 1049 mg Sodium

Beef

Beef Bourguignon

Serve this stew of tender, rich-flavoured beef with noodles or mashed potatoes.
For more colour (and to sneak in some extra veggies), try stirring in some
cooked carrots before serving.

Boneless beef blade steak, cut into 1 inch (2.5 cm) pieces	10 oz.	285 g
Salt	1/2 tsp.	2 mL
Pepper, just a pinch		
Cooking oil	1 tbsp.	15 mL
Small fresh white mushrooms	1 cup	250 mL
Pearl onions, peeled	3/4 cup	175 mL
Garlic clove, minced	1	1
(or 1/4 tsp., 1 mL, powder)		
All-purpose flour	2 tbsp.	30 mL
Dry (or alcohol-free) red wine	1/2 cup	125 mL
Prepared beef broth	1/2 cup	125 mL
Bay leaf	1	1

Chopped fresh parsley, for garnish

Sprinkle beef with salt and pepper. Heat cooking oil in large frying pan on medium-high. Add beef. Cook for about 4 minutes, stirring occasionally, until browned. Transfer beef to ungreased 1 quart (1 L) casserole with slotted spoon. Reduce heat to medium.

Add next 3 ingredients to same frying pan. Cook for about 5 minutes, stirring occasionally, until onion starts to soften.

Sprinkle with flour. Heat and stir for 1 minute. Slowly add wine and broth, stirring constantly until smooth. Heat and stir until boiling and thickened. Pour over beef. Add bay leaf. Stir. Bake, covered, in 325°F (160°C) oven for about 75 minutes until beef is tender. Discard bay leaf.

Garnish with parsley. Makes about 2 1/2 cups (625 mL). Serves 2.

1 serving: 451 Calories; 22.2 g Total Fat (10.0 g Mono, 2.7 g Poly, 6.2 g Sat); 94 mg Cholesterol;
21 g Carbohydrate; 1 g Fibre; 30 g Protein; 1045 mg Sodium

Nostalgic Mini-Meatloaf

If you're looking for the comfort of a good, old-fashioned meatloaf like Grandma used to make, this is the one! Serve with mashed potatoes, creamed corn and green veggies for the complete experience.

Ketchup	2 tbsp.	30 mL
Steak sauce	1/2 tsp.	2 mL
Large egg, fork-beaten	1	1
Crushed salted soda crackers	1/4 cup	60 mL
(about 8 crackers)		
Finely chopped onion	1/4 cup	60 mL
Prepared horseradish	2 tsp.	10 mL
Garlic clove, minced	1	1
Seasoned salt	1/2 tsp.	2 mL
Pepper	1/8 tsp.	0.5 mL
Lean ground beef	1/2 lb.	225 g

Combine ketchup and steak sauce in small cup.

Combine next 7 ingredients in medium bowl. Add beef. Mix well. Press into greased 6 x 3 1/2 x 2 inch (15 x 9 x 5 cm) foil loaf pan. Bake, uncovered, in 375°F (190°C) oven for 25 minutes. Spread ketchup mixture over meatloaf. Bake for about 25 minutes until fully cooked and internal temperature of beef reaches 160°F (71°C). Let stand in pan for 10 minutes. Cuts into 6 slices. Serves 2.

1 serving: 311 Calories; 14.6 g Total Fat (5.6 g Mono, 0.5 g Poly, 5.5 g Sat); 181 mg Cholesterol; 17 g Carbohydrate; 1 g Fibre; 27 g Protein; 694 mg Sodium

1. Beef Ale Penne, page 56
2. Curry Beef And Potato, page 45
3. Pineapple Beef Stir-Fry, page 43

Props courtesy of: Stokes
Corelle®
Danesco Inc.

Beef

Rosemary Cream Steak

Rosemary and beef have been used together for centuries. This recipe
celebrates these two fantastic ingredients to create one sumptuous steak.

Beef rib-eye steak, cut in half	1/2 lb.	225 g
Montreal steak spice	1/2 tsp.	2 mL
Olive (or cooking) oil	1 tsp.	5 mL
Olive (or cooking) oil	1 tsp.	5 mL
Sliced fresh white mushrooms	1 cup	250 mL
Prepared beef broth	1/2 cup	125 mL
Chopped fresh rosemary	2 tsp.	10 mL
Worcestershire sauce	1 tsp.	5 mL
Garlic powder	1/4 tsp.	1 mL
Sour cream	3 tbsp.	50 mL

Sprinkle steak with steak spice. Heat first amount of olive oil in medium
frying pan on medium-high. Add steak. Cook for about 2 minutes per
side until beef reaches desired doneness. Remove to serving plate. Cover
with foil. Let stand for 10 minutes. Wipe pan with paper towel. Reduce
heat to medium.

Add second amount of olive oil and mushrooms to same frying pan. Cook
for about 2 minutes until mushrooms are starting to brown.

Add next 4 ingredients. Stir. Cook, uncovered, for about 4 minutes until
fragrant and liquid is slightly reduced. Remove from heat.

Add sour cream. Stir. Spoon over steak. Serves 2.

1 serving: 238 Calories; 14.7 g Total Fat (5.8 g Mono, 0.9 g Poly, 5.7 g Sat); 75 mg Cholesterol;
3 g Carbohydrate; trace Fibre; 21 g Protein; 570 mg Sodium

1. Golden Bread Crown, page 130
2. Petite Pot Roast, page 46

Beef Ale Penne

Slow simmering results in tender beef and a smooth sauce. An English-style brown ale is particularly nice in this recipe.

Cooking oil	2 tsp.	10 mL
Boneless beef round steak, trimmed of fat, cut into 1/2 inch (12 mm) cubes	1/2 lb.	225 g
Coarsely chopped fresh white mushrooms	1 cup	250 mL
Coarsely chopped onion	1 cup	250 mL
Brown ale	2/3 cup	150 mL
Prepared beef broth	2/3 cup	150 mL
Worcestershire sauce	2 tsp.	10 mL
Brown sugar, packed	1 tsp.	5 mL
Dried thyme	1/4 tsp.	1 mL
Parsley flakes	1/4 tsp.	1 mL
Salt	1/2 tsp.	2 mL
Pepper, just a pinch		
Water	8 cups	2 L
Salt	1 tsp.	5 mL
Penne pasta	1 1/4 cups	30ww0 mL
Water	2 tbsp.	30 mL
Cornstarch	1 tbsp.	15 mL

Heat cooking oil in medium saucepan on medium-high. Add beef. Cook for about 3 minutes, stirring occasionally, until no longer pink. Reduce heat to medium.

Add mushrooms and onion. Cook for about 10 minutes, stirring often, until onion is softened and liquid is evaporated.

Add next 8 ingredients. Stir. Bring to a boil. Reduce heat to medium-low. Simmer, covered, for about 45 minutes until beef is tender.

Combine first amount of water and salt in large saucepan. Bring to a boil. Add pasta. Boil, uncovered, for 14 to 16 minutes, stirring occasionally, until tender but firm. Drain. Return to same pot. Cover to keep warm.

(continued on next page)

Beef

Stir second amount of water into cornstarch in small cup. Add to beef mixture. Heat and stir until boiling and thickened. Add pasta. Stir until coated. Makes about 3 1/2 cups (875 mL). Serves 2.

1 serving: 546 Calories; 9.8 g Total Fat (4.2 g Mono, 1.5 g Poly, 1.7 g Sat); 64 mg Cholesterol; 70 g Carbohydrate; 4 g Fibre; 37 g Protein; 853 mg Sodium

Pictured on page 53.

Beef Satay

These flavourful beef skewers work great as an appetizer or as a meal served with rice or noodles and a salad.

PEANUT SAUCE

Smooth peanut butter	1/2 cup	125 mL
Hot water	3 tbsp.	50 mL
Lime juice	1 tbsp.	15 mL
Soy sauce	1 tbsp.	15 mL
Brown sugar, packed	2 tsp.	10 mL
Finely grated ginger root	2 tsp.	10 mL
(or 1/2 tsp., 2 mL, ground ginger)		
Garlic clove, minced	1	1
(or 1/4 tsp., 1 mL, powder)		

SATAY

Beef strip loin steak (about 1 inch,	1/2 lb.	225 g
2.5 cm, thick), trimmed of fat		
Bamboo skewers (8 inches, 20 cm, each),	6	6
soaked in water for 10 minutes		
Salt	1/4 tsp.	1 mL
Pepper	1/4 tsp.	1 mL

Peanut Sauce: Whisk all 7 ingredients in small bowl until smooth. Makes about 3/4 cup (175 mL) sauce. Reserve 1/2 cup (125 mL) in small bowl.

Satay: Cut steak across the grain into 1/4 inch (6 mm) slices (see Tip, page 93). Thread accordion-style onto skewers. Sprinkle with salt and pepper. Arrange on greased broiler pan. Brush both sides with remaining Peanut Sauce. Broil on top rack in oven for about 2 minutes per side until starting to brown. Serve with reserved Peanut Sauce. Serves 2.

1 serving: 572 Calories; 40.5 g Total Fat (2.7 g Mono, 0.3 g Poly, 9.5 g Sat); 49 mg Cholesterol; 21 g Carbohydrate; 4 g Fibre; 39 g Protein; 1301 mg Sodium

Creamy Chicken Polenta

Wonderfully smooth polenta makes the perfect base for tender chicken in a creamy Parmesan sauce.

POLENTA		
Prepared chicken broth	1 cup	250 mL
Yellow cornmeal	1/3 cup	75 mL
Butter (or hard margarine)	1 tbsp.	15 mL

CHICKEN		
Butter (or hard margarine)	1 tbsp.	15 mL
All-purpose flour	1 tbsp.	15 mL
Salt	1/8 tsp.	0.5 mL
Pepper	1/8 tsp.	0.5 mL
Milk	1 cup	250 mL
Grated Parmesan cheese	1/3 cup	75 mL
Diced cooked chicken	1/4 cup	60 mL

Polenta: Measure broth into small saucepan. Bring to a boil. Reduce heat to medium. Slowly add cornmeal, stirring constantly. Add butter. Stir. Reduce heat to medium-low. Simmer, covered, for about 2 minutes, stirring often, until thickened.

Chicken: Melt butter in separate small saucepan on medium. Add next 3 ingredients. Heat and stir for 1 minute.

Slowly add milk, stirring constantly until smooth. Heat and stir until boiling and thickened. Remove from heat.

Add cheese and chicken. Stir until heated through. Spoon polenta onto 2 plates. Spoon chicken mixture over top. Serves 2.

1 serving: 366 Calories; 20.9 g Total Fat (4.2 g Mono, 1.1 g Poly, 12.5 g Sat); 73 mg Cholesterol; 27 g Carbohydrate; 1 g Fibre; 20 g Protein; 1671 mg Sodium

Poached Pesto Chicken

When time is of the essence, this dish is ready and on the table in short order. For those really time-crunched days, the chicken can be poached a day in advance and served cold, topped with the cheese and pesto.

Prepared chicken broth	1 1/2 cups	375 mL
Dry vermouth (or dry or alcohol-free white wine)	2 tbsp.	30 mL
Bay leaf	1	1
Boneless, skinless chicken breast halves (4 – 6 oz., 113 – 170 g, each)	2	2
Basil pesto	1 tbsp.	15 mL
Grated Asiago cheese	1 tbsp.	15 mL

Combine first 3 ingredients in small saucepan. Bring to a boil. Add chicken. Reduce heat to medium-low. Simmer, covered, for about 12 minutes until fully cooked and internal temperature reaches 170°F (77°C).

Remove 2 tsp. (10 mL) poaching liquid to small bowl. Add pesto and cheese. Stir. Transfer chicken with slotted spoon to individual plates. Spoon pesto mixture over top. Serves 2.

1 serving: 178 Calories; 6.4 g Total Fat (0.3 g Mono, 0.3 g Poly, 1.6 g Sat); 71 mg Cholesterol; trace Carbohydrate; trace Fibre; 28 g Protein; 174 mg Sodium

Paré Pointer

The lollipop could never win a fight—he was always licked.

Chicken Paella

This is not paella (pronounced pie-AY-yuh) as you usually know it; this version is made with orzo instead of rice. Great herb flavour in a colourful combo of chicken, sausage and veggies.

Cooking oil	1 tsp.	5 mL
Boneless, skinless chicken breast, cut into 1 1/2 inch (3.8 cm) pieces	6 oz.	170 g
Chicken (or turkey) sausage, cut into 1 1/2 inch (3.8 cm) pieces	4 oz.	113 g
Chopped red pepper	1/2 cup	125 mL
Finely chopped onion	1/4 cup	60 mL
Garlic clove, minced (or 1/4 tsp., 1 mL, powder)	1	1
Prepared chicken broth	1 1/2 cups	375 mL
Diced Roma (plum) tomatoes	1 cup	250 mL
Orzo	3/4 cup	175 mL
Worcestershire sauce	1 tsp.	5 mL
Dried oregano	1/2 tsp.	2 mL
Dried thyme	1/2 tsp.	2 mL
Frozen peas, thawed	1/2 cup	125 mL

Heat cooking oil in large frying pan on medium. Add chicken and sausage. Cook for about 8 minutes, stirring occasionally, until browned. Remove to plate with slotted spoon. Cover to keep warm.

Add next 3 ingredients to same frying pan. Cook for about 2 minutes, stirring often, until onion starts to brown.

Add next 6 ingredients, chicken and sausage. Stir. Bring to a boil. Cook for about 10 minutes, stirring often, until liquid is absorbed and pasta is almost tender.

Sprinkle with peas. Remove from heat. Let stand, covered, for 5 minutes. Stir. Makes about 3 1/2 cups (875 mL). Serves 2.

1 serving: 562 Calories; 13.2 g Total Fat (4.3 g Mono, 3.3 g Poly, 2.7 g Sat); 102 mg Cholesterol; 65 g Carbohydrate; 7 g Fibre; 46 g Protein; 1636 mg Sodium

Pesto-Stuffed Chicken

A delightful, moderately spicy homemade pesto is tucked inside tender chicken breasts. Cooking the chicken in foil packets makes for easy cleanup and convenient serving!

Finely chopped fresh parsley	1/3 cup	75 mL
Finely chopped pine nuts, toasted	2 tbsp.	30 mL
(see Tip, page 103)		
Olive (or cooking) oil	1 tbsp.	15 mL
Small garlic clove, minced	1	1
(or 1/8 tsp., 0.5 mL, powder)		
Liquid honey	1/2 tsp.	2 mL
Finely chopped chipotle pepper in	1/2 tsp.	2 mL
adobo sauce (see Tip, page 40)		
Grated orange zest	1/2 tsp.	2 mL
Boneless, skinless chicken breast halves	2	2
(4 – 6 oz., 113 – 170 g, each)		
Cooking spray		
Seasoned salt	1/2 tsp.	2 mL

Combine first 7 ingredients in small bowl.

Cut deep pocket in thickest part of each chicken breast almost, but not quite, through to other side. Spoon parsley mixture into pocket. Spray chicken with cooking spray. Sprinkle with seasoned salt. Place 1 chicken breast in centre of large piece of foil. Fold edges of foil together over chicken to enclose. Fold ends to seal completely. Repeat with remaining chicken breast. Place packets, seam-side up, on baking sheet. Bake in 450°F (230°C) oven for about 20 minutes until fully cooked and internal temperature of chicken reaches 170°F (77°C). Serves 2.

1 serving: 268 Calories; 16.6 g Total Fat (7.9 g Mono, 4.7 g Poly, 2.4 g Sat); 66 mg Cholesterol; 4 g Carbohydrate; 1 g Fibre; 26 g Protein; 419 mg Sodium

Pictured on front cover.

Roast Cornish Hen

A complete Sunday dinner, including tender potatoes that have the gravy cooked right in. Try cooking in a fancier roasting pan or baking dish so you can transfer your dinner right from the oven to the table, without disturbing the attractive browning that forms on the potatoes.

Baby potatoes, cut into 1/8 inch (3 mm) slices	2 cups	500 mL
Thinly sliced onion	1 cup	250 mL
Olive (or cooking) oil	1 tsp.	5 mL
Salt	1/4 tsp.	1 mL
Pepper	1/8 tsp.	0.5 mL
Sprigs of fresh thyme	3	3
Cornish hen	1 1/2 lbs.	680 g
Olive (or cooking) oil	1/2 tsp.	2 mL
Chili powder	1/2 tsp.	2 mL
Salt	1/8 tsp.	0.5 mL
Pepper	1/8 tsp.	0.5 mL
Chopped fresh thyme	1 tsp.	5 mL

Toss first 5 ingredients in medium bowl. Transfer to greased small roasting pan.

Place thyme sprigs in body cavity of hen. Tie legs together with butcher's string. Fold wings under body. Place, breast-side up, over potato mixture.

Rub second amount of olive oil over surface of hen. Combine next 3 ingredients in small cup. Sprinkle over hen. Cook, uncovered, in 425°F (220°C) oven for about 30 minutes until starting to turn golden. Reduce heat to 375°F (190°C). Cook, covered, for about 20 minutes until golden brown and meat thermometer inserted into thickest part of breast reads 180°F (82°C). Transfer hen to serving plate. Cover with foil. Let stand for 10 minutes before carving.

Sprinkle potato with thyme. Serves 2.

1 serving: 613 Calories; 32.8 g Total Fat (15.4 g Mono, 6.3 g Poly, 8.6 g Sat); 211 mg Cholesterol; 36 g Carbohydrate; 3 g Fibre; 40 g Protein; 551 mg Sodium

Pictured on page 144.

Arugula Chicken

Load up on fresh Italian flavours with this fun combination of warm chicken and sauce over peppery arugula.

Boneless, skinless chicken breast halves (4 – 6 oz., 113 – 170 g, each)	2	2
Salt, sprinkle		
Pepper, sprinkle		
Olive oil	1 tsp.	5 mL
Jar of marinated artichoke hearts, drained and coarsely chopped	6 oz.	170 mL
Prepared bruschetta topping	1/2 cup	125 mL
Black olive tapenade	1 tbsp.	15 mL
Prepared chicken broth	1/2 cup	125 mL
Grated Parmesan cheese	1/4 cup	60 mL
Chopped fresh basil (or 3/4 tsp., 4 mL, dried)	1 tbsp.	15 mL
Arugula leaves, lightly packed	1 1/2 cups	375 mL

Cut each chicken breast in half horizontally to make 2 thin, flat pieces. Sprinkle with salt and pepper. Heat olive oil in large frying pan on medium-high. Add chicken. Cook for about 2 minutes per side until browned and no longer pink inside. Transfer to plate. Cover to keep warm.

Add next 3 ingredients to same frying pan. Heat and stir for about 1 minute until fragrant. Add broth. Stir. Cook for about 3 minutes, stirring occasionally, until broth is reduced by half. Remove from heat.

Add cheese and basil. Stir.

Arrange arugula on 2 plates. Arrange chicken over arugula. Top with artichoke mixture. Serves 2.

1 serving: 329 Calories; 16.1 g Total Fat (3.0 g Mono, 1.3 g Poly, 3.5 g Sat); 76 mg Cholesterol; 11 g Carbohydrate; trace Fibre; 33 g Protein; 1336 mg Sodium

Chicken Curry

Curry in a hurry! This simple chicken dish will cure your curry cravings in no time.

Cooking oil	1 tsp.	5 mL
Boneless, skinless chicken thighs	4	4
(about 3 oz., 85 g, each)		
Chopped onion	1/2 cup	125 mL
Hot curry paste	2 tsp.	10 mL
Garlic clove, minced	1	1
(or 1/4 tsp., 1 mL, powder)		
Finely grated ginger root	1/2 tsp.	2 mL
(or 1/8 tsp., 0.5 mL, ground ginger)		
Salt	1/4 tsp.	1 mL
Pepper	1/8 tsp.	0.5 mL
Applesauce	1/2 cup	125 mL
Plain yogurt	1/3 cup	75 mL
Chopped fresh cilantro or parsley	1 tsp.	5 mL

Heat cooking oil in medium frying pan on medium. Add chicken. Cook for about 3 minutes per side until browned. Transfer to plate. Cover to keep warm.

Add next 6 ingredients to same frying pan. Cook for about 5 minutes, stirring often, until onion is softened.

Add applesauce. Stir. Add chicken. Stir until coated. Reduce heat to medium-low. Cook, covered, for about 5 minutes until chicken is fully cooked and internal temperature reaches 170°F (77°C). Remove from heat.

Add yogurt. Stir. Sprinkle with cilantro. Serves 2.

1 serving: 347 Calories; 16.0 g Total Fat (6.2 g Mono, 3.6 g Poly, 4.0 g Sat); 113 mg Cholesterol; 16 g Carbohydrate; 1 g Fibre; 34 g Protein; 587 mg Sodium

Maple Balsamic Chicken

An absolutely delicious chicken dish with rich, warming sweet-and-sour flavours in a jewel-toned sauce. Pairs particularly well with roasted veggies.

Olive (or cooking) oil	1 1/2 tsp.	7 mL
Boneless, skinless chicken breast halves	2	2
(4 – 6 oz., 113 – 170 g, each)		
Chopped fresh rosemary	1 tsp.	5 mL
(or 1/4 tsp., 1 mL, dried, crushed)		
Salt, sprinkle		
Pepper, sprinkle		
Prepared chicken broth	3/4 cup	175 mL
Balsamic vinegar	2 tbsp.	30 mL
Maple (or maple-flavoured) syrup	2 tbsp.	30 mL
Coarsely ground pepper	1 tsp.	5 mL
Chopped fresh rosemary	1/2 tsp.	2 mL
(or 1/8 tsp., 0.5 mL, dried, crushed)		
Cold butter	1 tbsp.	15 mL

Heat olive oil in medium frying pan on medium-high. Add chicken. Sprinkle with next 3 ingredients. Cook for 2 to 3 minutes per side until browned.

Add next 5 ingredients. Bring to a boil. Reduce heat to medium-low. Cook, covered, for 12 to 15 minutes until chicken is fully cooked and internal temperature reaches 170°F (77°C). Transfer to plate. Cover to keep warm.

Heat and stir broth mixture for about 2 minutes until reduced by half. Add butter. Stir until melted. Pour over chicken. Serves 2.

1 serving: 291 Calories; 13.1 g Total Fat (5.4 g Mono, 1.7 g Poly, 5.2 g Sat); 81 mg Cholesterol; 17 g Carbohydrate; trace Fibre; 25 g Protein; 661 mg Sodium

Paré Pointer

Bees always have sticky hair because they use honeycombs.

Turkey Shepherd's Pie

Though it may appear involved, this recipe can be put together in about the same amount of time as it takes to make mashed potatoes—and you can set the table, toss a salad, light the candles and enjoy a drink while it's baking!

Cubed peeled potato	1 cup	250 mL
Salt	1/4 tsp.	1 mL
Prepared chicken broth	2 tbsp.	30 mL
Milk	1 tbsp.	15 mL
Ground sage, sprinkle		
Pepper, sprinkle		
Cooking oil	1 tsp.	5 mL
Finely chopped fresh white mushrooms	1/4 cup	60 mL
Finely chopped onion	1/4 cup	60 mL
Grated carrot	1/4 cup	60 mL
Finely diced celery	2 tbsp.	30 mL
Finely diced green pepper	2 tbsp.	30 mL
Extra-lean ground turkey breast	1/2 lb.	225 g
All-purpose flour	1 tbsp.	15 mL
Ground sage	1/4 tsp.	1 mL
Salt	1/8 tsp.	0.5 mL
Pepper, sprinkle		
Prepared chicken broth	1/2 cup	125 mL

Pour water into small saucepan until about 1 inch (2.5 cm) deep. Add potato and salt. Cover. Bring to a boil. Reduce heat to medium. Boil gently for 12 to 15 minutes until tender. Drain. Return to same pot.

Add next 4 ingredients. Mash.

Heat cooking oil in medium frying pan on medium. Add next 5 ingredients. Cook for about 5 minutes, stirring often, until onion is softened.

Add turkey. Scramble-fry for about 5 minutes until turkey is no longer pink.

(continued on next page)

Add next 4 ingredients. Heat and stir for 1 minute. Slowly add broth, stirring constantly until boiling and thickened. Transfer to ungreased 1 quart (1 L) casserole. Spoon potato mixture over top. Spread evenly. Bake, uncovered, in 350°F (175°C) oven for about 30 minutes until starting to brown. Serves 2.

1 serving: 262 Calories; 5.0 g Total Fat (1.6 g Mono, 0.9 g Poly, 0.6 g Sat); 45 mg Cholesterol; 26 g Carbohydrate; 4 g Fibre; 31 g Protein; 699 mg Sodium

Sweet-And-Sour Meatballs

Familiar sweet-and-sour flavours fill this Asian-inspired dish. Best served over jasmine rice.

Fine dry bread crumbs	2 tbsp.	30 mL
Finely chopped onion	1 tbsp.	15 mL
Soy sauce	1 tbsp.	15 mL
Sesame oil (for flavour)	1/2 tsp.	2 mL
Garlic powder	1/8 tsp.	0.5 mL
Pepper, sprinkle		
Lean ground turkey thigh	1/2 lb.	225 g
Sweet-and-sour sauce	3/4 cup	175 mL
Finely chopped green pepper	2 tbsp.	30 mL

Combine first 6 ingredients in small bowl. Add turkey. Mix well. Roll into twelve 1 inch (2.5 cm) balls. Arrange on greased baking sheet with sides. Bake in 350°F (175°C) oven for about 15 minutes until fully cooked and internal temperature reaches 175°F (80°C).

Heat sweet-and-sour sauce and green pepper in small saucepan on medium for about 2 minutes, stirring often, until pepper is tender-crisp. Add meatballs. Stir until coated. Serves 2.

1 serving: 287 Calories; 6.1 g Total Fat (0 g Mono, trace Poly, trace Sat); 45 mg Cholesterol; 31 g Carbohydrate; trace Fibre; 30 g Protein; 1121 mg Sodium

Balsamic Soy Turkey

Balsamic vinegar and soy sauce may seem like an unusual pairing, but they go together surprisingly well!

Rice stick noodles	4 oz.	113 g
Boiling water		
Cooking oil	1/2 tsp.	2 mL
Cooking oil	2 tsp.	10 mL
Sliced onion	1/2 cup	125 mL
Garlic clove, minced	1	1
(or 1/4 tsp., 1 mL, powder)		
Boneless, skinless turkey breast steak	1	1
(about 6 oz., 170 g), cut into 1/4 inch		
(6 mm) slices (see Tip, page 93)		
Sliced red pepper	1/2 cup	125 mL
Grated carrot	1/3 cup	75 mL
Balsamic vinegar	2 tbsp.	30 mL
Soy sauce	1 tbsp.	15 mL
Finely grated ginger root	1 tsp.	5 mL
(or 1/4 tsp., 1 mL, ground ginger)		
Granulated sugar	1 tsp.	5 mL
Chili paste (sambal oelek)	1/4 tsp.	1 mL

Put noodles into medium heatproof bowl. Add boiling water to cover. Let stand, covered, for about 20 minutes until noodles are tender. Drain.

Drizzle with first amount of cooking oil. Toss until coated. Cover to keep warm.

Heat second amount of cooking oil in medium frying pan on medium. Add onion and garlic. Cook for about 4 minutes, stirring often, until onion starts to soften.

Add turkey. Cook for about 3 minutes, stirring occasionally, until no longer pink.

Add red pepper and carrot. Cook for about 2 minutes, stirring occasionally, until red pepper is tender-crisp.

(continued on next page)

Chicken & Turkey

Add remaining 5 ingredients. Heat and stir until boiling. Add to noodles. Toss. Makes about 3 1/2 cups (875 mL). Serves 2.

1 serving: 407 Calories; 7.5 g Total Fat (3.5 g Mono, 1.9 g Poly, 1 g Sat); 34 mg Cholesterol; 61 g Carbohydrate; 3 g Fibre; 25 g Protein; 843 mg Sodium

Pictured on page 71 and on back cover.

Grilled Turkey Patties

Simple, yet satisfying—these moist turkey patties are given lots of flavour with the addition of a few basic ingredients. Serve as-is or in onion buns with all your favourite burger toppings.

Large flake rolled oats	1/3 cup	75 mL
Sun-dried tomato and oregano dressing	3 tbsp.	50 mL
Sliced green onion	2 tbsp.	30 mL
Lean ground turkey thigh	1/2 lb.	225 g
Barbecue sauce	2 tbsp.	30 mL

Combine first 3 ingredients in medium bowl. Add turkey. Mix well. Let stand for about 10 minutes until rolled oats are softened. Divide in half. Shape each portion into 4 inch (10 cm) diameter patty.

Preheat gas barbecue to medium-high (see Tip, below). Brush patties with barbecue sauce. Cook on greased grill for about 5 minutes per side until fully cooked and internal temperature reaches 175°F (80°C). Makes 2 patties.

1 patty: 294 Calories; 16 g Total Fat (4.3 g Mono, 3.5 g Poly, 3.9 g Sat); 97 mg Cholesterol; 14 g Carbohydrate; 2 g Fibre; 23 g Protein; 527 mg Sodium

 tip   Too cold to barbecue? Use the broiler instead! Your food should cook in about the same length of time—and remember to turn or baste as directed. Set your oven rack so that the food is about 3 to 4 inches (7.5 to 10 cm) away from the top element—for most ovens, this is the top rack.

Chinese BBQ Chicken

Sweet and a little spicy, these tender glazed chicken thighs are accented with the lively crunch of radish and green onion. Serve with steamed rice and stir-fried veggies for a complete meal.

Chinese barbecue sauce (Char Siu sauce)	3 tbsp.	50 mL
Sweet chili sauce	1 tbsp.	15 mL
Garlic clove, minced	1	1
(or 1/4 tsp., 1 mL, powder)		
Boneless, skinless chicken thighs	4	4
(about 3 oz., 85 g, each)		
Julienned radish (see Tip, page 32)	1/4 cup	60 mL
Sliced green onion	1 tbsp.	15 mL

Combine first 3 ingredients in medium resealable freezer bag.

Add chicken. Seal bag. Turn until coated. Let stand in refrigerator for 1 hour, turning occasionally. Drain and discard barbecue sauce mixture. Preheat gas barbecue to medium-high (see Tip, page 69). Cook chicken on well-greased grill for about 5 minutes per side until fully cooked and internal temperature reaches 170°F (77°C). Remove to serving plate.

Sprinkle with radish and green onion. Serves 2.

1 serving: 298 Calories; 13.0 g Total Fat (4.9 g Mono, 3.0 g Poly, 3.6 g Sat); 112 mg Cholesterol; 9 g Carbohydrate; trace Fibre; 31 g Protein; 456 mg Sodium

Pictured at right and on back cover.

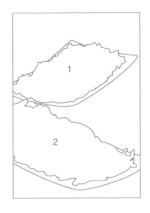

1. Chinese BBQ Chicken, above
2. Balsamic Soy Turkey, page 68

Props courtesy of: Danesco Inc.

Chicken & Turkey

Shrimp And Avocado Pizzas

Pizza gets an uptown makeover in the form of this not-too-cheesy pie.
Shrimp, avocado and basil make for unique, yet delicious toppings
on this sauce-free pizza.

Flour tortillas (9 inch, 22 cm, diameter)	2	2
Olive (or cooking) oil	1 tbsp.	15 mL
Garlic clove, minced	1	1
(or 1/4 tsp., 1 mL, powder)		
Grated Parmesan cheese	1/2 cup	125 mL
Cooked salad shrimp	4 oz.	113 g
(about 3/4 cup, 175 mL)		
Roasted red pepper, cut into strips,	1/4 cup	60 mL
blotted dry		
Diced avocado	2/3 cup	150 mL
Chopped fresh basil	1 tbsp.	15 mL

Lemon wedges, for garnish

Place tortillas on greased baking sheet. Combine olive oil and garlic in small cup. Spread over tortillas.

Scatter next 3 ingredients, in order given, over tortillas. Bake in 425°F (220°C) oven for about 10 minutes until edges are golden. Transfer to serving plates.

Sprinkle avocado and basil over top.

Garnish with lemon wedges. Serves 2.

1 serving: 509 Calories; 32.2 g Total Fat (13.7 g Mono, 4.8 g Poly, 8.7 g Sat); 97 mg Cholesterol; 32 g Carbohydrate; 5 g Fibre; 25 g Protein; 1034 mg Sodium

1. Shrimp And Scallop Orzo, page 74
2. Lemon Dill Salmon In Puff Pastry, page 75
3. Fiesta Shrimp, page 83

Shrimp And Scallop Orzo

A deliciously light one-dish meal. Quick and easy to prepare after a long day at work.

Water	4 cups	1 L
Salt	1/2 tsp.	2 mL
Orzo	1/2 cup	125 mL
Butter (or hard margarine)	1 tbsp.	15 mL
Cooking oil	1 tbsp.	15 mL
Small bay scallops	4 oz.	113 g
Uncooked medium shrimp	4 oz.	113 g
(peeled and deveined)		
Dry (or alcohol-free) white wine	1/4 cup	60 mL
Chopped green onion	2 tbsp.	30 mL
Lemon juice	1 tbsp.	15 mL
Garlic clove, minced	1	1
(or 1/4 tsp., 1 mL, powder)		
Grated Romano cheese	3 tbsp.	50 mL
Chopped fresh basil	1 tbsp.	15 mL

Combine water and salt in large saucepan. Bring to a boil. Add pasta. Boil, uncovered, for about 8 minutes, stirring occasionally, until tender but firm. Drain. Return to same pot. Cover to keep warm.

Heat butter and cooking oil in large frying pan on medium. Add next 6 ingredients. Cook for about 4 minutes, stirring occasionally, until scallops are opaque and shrimp turn pink. Remove from heat.

Add cheese, basil and pasta. Stir gently. Makes about 2 1/4 cups (550 mL). Serves 2.

1 serving: 437 Calories; 17.0 g Total Fat (6.4 g Mono, 2.8 g Poly, 6.1 g Sat); 130 mg Cholesterol; 36 g Carbohydrate; 1 g Fibre; 30 g Protein; 332 mg Sodium

Pictured on page 72.

Lemon Dill Salmon In Puff Pastry

The classic flavours of lemon and dill pair perfectly with salmon in crisp puff pastry. An inventive meal idea for a romantic dinner.

Mayonnaise	1/4 cup	60 mL
Sour cream	1/4 cup	60 mL
Chopped fresh dill	2 tbsp.	30 mL
Garlic clove, minced	1	1
(or 1/4 tsp., 1 mL, powder)		
Dijon mustard	1 tsp.	5 mL
Lemon juice	1 tsp.	5 mL
Grated lemon zest	1/2 tsp.	2 mL
Puff pastry patty shells	2	2
Salmon fillet, skin removed	10 oz.	285 g
Lemon slices, about 1/4 inch (6 mm) thick	2	2
Onion slices, about 1/4 inch (6 mm) thick	2	2

Chopped fresh dill, for garnish

Combine first 7 ingredients in medium bowl. Chill, covered, for 1 hour to blend flavours.

Place pastry shells on baking sheet. Bake on centre rack in 400°F (205°C) oven for about 18 minutes until golden. Transfer to serving plates.

Place fillet on separate greased baking sheet. Arrange lemon and onion slices over fillet. Bake in 400°F (205°C) oven for about 13 minutes until fillet flakes easily when tested with fork. Discard lemon and onion slices. Break salmon into small pieces with fork. Add to sour cream mixture. Makes about 1 1/2 cups (375 mL). Fill shells with salmon mixture.

Garnish with dill. Serve immediately. Serves 2.

1 serving: 717 Calories; 52.3 g Total Fat (26.0 g Mono, 10.2 g Poly, 12.3 g Sat); 113 mg Cholesterol; 27 g Carbohydrate; 1 g Fibre; 33 g Protein; 414 mg Sodium

Pictured on page 72.

Asian Shrimp-Stuffed Sole

Can't decide between fish or shrimp? Why not serve both? Delicate sole fillets
are stuffed with a filling of moist shrimp, vibrant ginger and chili.

White bread slice	1	1
Egg white (large)	1	1
Uncooked shrimp (peeled and deveined)	4 oz.	113 g
Finely chopped onion	1 tbsp.	15 mL
Sweet chili sauce	2 tsp.	10 mL
Chopped fresh basil	1 tsp.	5 mL
(or 1/4 tsp., 1 mL, dried)		
Small garlic clove, minced	1	1
(or 1/8 tsp., 0.5 mL, powder)		
Grated ginger root	1/2 tsp.	2 mL
(or 1/8 tsp., 1 mL, ground ginger)		
Salt	1/8 tsp.	0.5 mL
Sole fillets, any small bones removed	4	4
(about 2 oz., 57 g, each)		
Sake (rice wine)	1/4 cup	60 mL
Sliced green onion	1 tbsp.	15 mL
Sesame seeds, toasted (see Tip, page 103)	1 tsp.	5 mL

Process bread in blender or food processor until coarse crumbs form.
Transfer to small bowl.

Process next 8 ingredients in blender or food processor until shrimp is
coarsely chopped. Add bread crumbs. Process until combined.

Arrange fillets, dark-side up, on work surface. Spoon about 1/4 cup (60 mL)
shrimp mixture onto centre of each fillet. Starting with thinnest end, roll up
to enclose filling. Arrange, seam-side down, in greased 1 quart (1 L)
baking dish.

Pour sake over fillets. Bake, covered, in 375°F (190°C) oven for about
30 minutes until fish flakes easily when tested with fork. Transfer fillets
with slotted spoon to serving dish. Discard liquid.

Sprinkle with green onion and sesame seeds. Makes 4 stuffed fillets. Serves 2.

1 serving: 227 Calories; 3.5 g Total Fat (0.8 g Mono, 1.3 g Poly, 0.7 g Sat); 141 mg Cholesterol;
10 g Carbohydrate; 1 g Fibre; 36 g Protein; 464 mg Sodium

Fish & Seafood

Creamy Seafood Casserole

This saucy seafood treat is best served over rice to catch every last bit of the flavourful sauce.

Butter (or hard margarine)	1 tbsp.	15 mL
Chopped onion	1/3 cup	75 mL
Salt	1/8 tsp.	0.5 mL
All-purpose flour	1 tbsp.	15 mL
Milk	1/2 cup	125 mL
Haddock fillet, any small bones removed, cut into 1 inch (2.5 cm) pieces	4 oz.	113 g
Large sea scallops, cut in half horizontally	2 oz.	57 g
Uncooked medium shrimp (peeled and deveined)	2 oz.	57 g
Chopped fresh dill (or 1/4 tsp., 1 mL, dried)	1 tsp.	5 mL
Chopped fresh parsley (or 1/4 tsp., 1 mL, flakes)	1 tsp.	5 mL
Pepper, just a pinch		
Grated Parmesan cheese	2 tbsp.	30 mL

Melt butter in small saucepan on medium. Add onion and salt. Cook for about 3 minutes, stirring often, until onion is softened.

Add flour. Heat and stir for 1 minute. Slowly add milk, stirring constantly until smooth. Heat and stir until boiling and thickened.

Add next 6 ingredients. Stir. Transfer to greased 2 cup (500 mL) baking dish.

Sprinkle with cheese. Bake, uncovered, in 375°F (190°C) oven for about 20 minutes until cheese is golden and mixture is bubbling around edges. Makes about 1 2/3 cups (400 mL). Serves 2.

1 serving: 234 Calories; 9.3 g Total Fat (2.4 g Mono, 0.7 g Poly, 5.4 g Sat); 108 mg Cholesterol; 10 g Carbohydrate; trace Fibre; 27 g Protein; 463 mg Sodium

Lemon Tarragon Salmon

Delicate salmon fillets are blanketed in a creamy herb sauce. Serve with lemon wedges for an added burst of citrus freshness.

Prepared vegetable broth	1 cup	250 mL
Lemon slice, about 1/4 inch (6 mm) thick	1	1
Bay leaf	1	1
Dried tarragon	1/8 tsp.	0.5 mL
Fresh (or frozen, thawed) salmon fillets (about 4 oz., 113 g, each), skin removed	2	2
Water	1 tsp.	5 mL
Cornstarch	1 tsp.	5 mL
Sour cream	1/4 cup	60 mL
Pepper, just a pinch		

Combine first 4 ingredients in small frying pan. Bring to a boil. Reduce heat to medium.

Add fillets. Cook, partially covered, for about 4 minutes until fish flakes easily when tested with fork. Remove fillets to serving plate with slotted spoon. Cover to keep warm. Strain liquid through sieve into small saucepan. Discard solids. Boil liquid for about 6 minutes until reduced by half.

Stir water into cornstarch in small cup. Slowly add to pan, stirring constantly until boiling and thickened.

Add sour cream and pepper. Cook and stir until heated through. Do not boil. Pour over fillets. Serves 2.

1 serving: 279 Calories; 17.3 g Total Fat (6.6 g Mono, 2.6 g Poly, 6.1 g Sat); 87 mg Cholesterol; 5 g Carbohydrate; 1 g Fibre; 24 g Protein; 297 mg Sodium

Potato Fish Cakes

These fish cakes are sure to please. They're crispy on the outside, soft on the inside and filled with the unexpected flavour of Swiss cheese. Serve with sour cream and a squeeze of lemon.

Cubed peeled potato	2 cups	500 mL
Cooking oil	1 tsp.	5 mL
Haddock fillets, any small bones removed	1/2 lb.	225 g
Grated Swiss cheese	1/2 cup	125 mL
Chopped fresh chives	1 tbsp.	15 mL
Salt	1/2 tsp.	2 mL
Pepper	1/4 tsp.	1 mL
Cooking oil	3 tbsp.	50 mL

Pour water into large saucepan until about 1 inch (2.5 cm) deep. Add potato. Cover. Bring to a boil. Reduce heat to medium. Boil gently for 12 to 15 minutes until tender. Drain. Mash.

Heat first amount of cooking oil in medium frying pan on medium. Add fillets. Cook for about 3 minutes per side until fish flakes easily when tested with fork. Remove from pan. Break into small pieces. Add to mashed potato.

Add next 4 ingredients. Stir. Shape into four 3 inch (7.5 cm) diameter cakes.

Heat second amount of cooking oil in same frying pan on medium-high. Add cakes. Cook for about 3 minutes per side until golden brown. Remove to paper towels to drain. Serve immediately. Makes 4 fish cakes. Serves 2.

1 serving: 545 Calories; 31.7 g Total Fat (13.5 g Mono, 7.1 g Poly, 6.8 g Sat); 90 mg Cholesterol; 32 g Carbohydrate; 3 g Fibre; 31 g Protein; 730 mg Sodium

Paré Pointer

An electrician never tires of wiring for money.

Parmesan Snapper

This dish will leave you wondering what's better—the fancy presentation or the deliciously savoury taste. Regardless, you and your dinner companion are sure to enjoy.

Grated Parmesan cheese	2 tbsp.	30 mL
Mayonnaise	2 tbsp.	30 mL
Chili powder	1 tsp.	5 mL
Worcestershire sauce	1/4 tsp.	1 mL
Garlic powder	1/8 tsp.	0.5 mL
Pepper	1/8 tsp.	0.5 mL
Snapper fillets (4 – 5 oz., 113 – 140 g, each), skin and any small bones removed	2	2

Combine first 6 ingredients in small cup.

Place fillets on greased baking sheet. Spread cheese mixture evenly over fillets. Bake in 425°F (220°C) oven for about 8 minutes until fish flakes easily when tested with fork. Serves 2.

1 serving: 330 Calories; 18.0 g Total Fat (7.2 g Mono, 3.2 g Poly, 6.7 g Sat); 70 mg Cholesterol; 4 g Carbohydrate; trace Fibre; 36 g Protein; 750 mg Sodium

Lemon Pesto Seafood Skewers

You can easily justify firing up the barbecue for a couple of skewers if you grill some potatoes and vegetables at the same time to make a complete meal.

Lemon juice	1 tbsp.	15 mL
Sun-dried tomato pesto	1 tsp.	5 mL
Uncooked large shrimp (peeled and deveined), about 4 oz., 113 g	8	8
Large sea scallops (about 4 oz., 113 g)	6	6
Bamboo skewers (8 inches, 20 cm, each), soaked in water for 10 minutes	2	2

(continued on next page)

Fish & Seafood

Combine lemon juice and pesto in small cup.

Thread shrimp and scallops alternately onto skewers. Preheat gas barbecue to medium-high (see Tip, page 69). Cook on greased grill for about 2 minutes per side until shrimp turn pink and scallops are opaque. Brush with pesto mixture. Serves 2.

1 serving: 83 Calories; 0.9 g Total Fat (0.1 g Mono, 0.3 g Poly, 0.1 g Sat); 61 mg Cholesterol; 3 g Carbohydrate; trace Fibre; 15 g Protein; 159 mg Sodium

Curry Shrimp

Share the wealth. This rich and creamy coconut curry dish includes an abundance of delicious sauce, perfect for serving over rice or pasta.

Cooking oil	1 tsp.	5 mL
Chopped onion	1/2 cup	125 mL
Small garlic clove, minced	1	1
(or 1/8 tsp., 0.5 mL, powder)		
Thinly sliced red pepper	1/2 cup	125 mL
Curry paste	2 tsp.	10 mL
Finely grated ginger root	1/2 tsp.	2 mL
Salt	1/4 tsp.	1 mL
Coconut milk (or reconstituted	1 cup	250 mL
from powder)		
Uncooked large shrimp	6 oz.	170 mL
(peeled and deveined)		

Heat cooking oil in medium frying pan on medium. Add onion and garlic. Cook for about 5 minutes, stirring often, until onion is softened.

Add next 4 ingredients. Heat and stir for about 2 minutes until fragrant.

Add coconut milk. Stir. Bring to a boil. Add shrimp. Cook for about 3 minutes until shrimp turn pink. Makes about 2 cups (500 mL). Serves 2.

1 serving: 389 Calories; 30.5 g Total Fat (2.7 g Mono, 1.6 g Poly, 23.5 g Sat); 129 mg Cholesterol; 12 g Carbohydrate; 1 g Fibre; 21 g Protein; 613 mg Sodium

Sweet-Spiced Halibut

Aromatic spices, sweet honey and vanilla perfectly complement mild-flavoured halibut.

Liquid honey	1 tbsp.	15 mL
Ground cumin	1 1/2 tsp.	7 mL
Chili powder	1 tsp.	5 mL
Vanilla extract	1/2 tsp.	2 mL
Ground turmeric	1/4 tsp.	1 mL
Ground allspice	1/8 tsp.	0.5 mL
Salt	1/8 tsp.	0.5 mL
Halibut fillet, skin-on	1	1
(about 1/2 lb., 225 g)		
Lime wedges	2	2

Combine first 7 ingredients in small bowl. Brush over fillet. Preheat gas barbecue to high (see Tip, page 69). Cook fillet, skin-side up, on well-greased grill for 4 minutes. Turn. Cook for about 2 minutes until fish flakes easily when tested with fork.

Squeeze lime wedges over fillet. Serves 2.

1 serving: 174 Calories; 3.2 g Total Fat (0.9 g Mono, 0.9 g Poly, 0.4 g Sat); 36 mg Cholesterol; 10 g Carbohydrate; 1 g Fibre; 24 g Protein; 224 mg Sodium

Smoked Salmon-Crusted Halibut

If the title of this recipe has you wondering, we assure you, it is possible! Smoked salmon cream cheese actually complements mild halibut perfectly!

Halibut fillets, skin-on	2	2
(4 – 5 oz., 113 – 140 g, each)		
Smoked salmon cream cheese	1/3 cup	75 mL
Fine dry bread crumbs	3 tbsp.	50 mL
Lemon juice	1/2 tsp.	2 mL
Chopped fresh dill (or 1/4 tsp., 1 mL, dried)	1 tsp.	5 mL
Cayenne pepper, sprinkle		

(continued on next page)

Fish & Seafood

Place fillets, skin-side down, on greased 9 inch (22 cm) pie plate.

Combine remaining 5 ingredients in small bowl. Spread evenly over fillets. Bake in 450°F (230°C) oven for about 12 minutes until golden and fish flakes easily when tested with fork. Serves 2.

1 serving: 258 Calories; 11.1 g Total Fat (1.1 g Mono, 0.9 g Poly, 5.8 g Sat); 63 mg Cholesterol; 9 g Carbohydrate; trace Fibre; 28 g Protein; 335 mg Sodium

Fiesta Shrimp

This dish is sure to get the party started, even if there are only two of you! Tequila adds flaming fun to this special seafood recipe. Best served over rice.

Butter (or hard margarine)	1 tbsp.	15 mL
Uncooked large shrimp	10 oz.	285 g
(peeled and deveined)		
Salt	1/4 tsp.	1 mL
Pepper	1/8 tsp.	0.5 mL
Tequila	2 tbsp.	30 mL
Sour cream	1/4 cup	60 mL
Sliced green onion	1 tbsp.	15 mL

Melt butter in medium frying pan on medium-high. Add next 3 ingredients. Cook shrimp for about 2 minutes, stirring occasionally, until just starting to turn pink. Remove from heat.

Add tequila. Carefully ignite tequila with match. Gently stir for about 10 seconds until flame extinguishes.

Add sour cream and green onion. Stir. Serves 2.

1 serving: 296 Calories; 13.3 g Total Fat (3.3 g Mono, 1.4 g Poly, 7.3 g Sat); 243 mg Cholesterol; 2.7 g Carbohydrate; trace Fibre; 30 g Protein; 557 mg Sodium

Pictured on page 72.

Moroccan Meatballs

Tender lamb, exotic spice combinations and dried fruit are typical of Moroccan cuisine. Serve these meatballs with couscous to keep the theme going.

Chopped fresh parsley	1/4 cup	60 mL
(or 1 tbsp., 15 mL, flakes)		
Currants	2 tbsp.	30 mL
Fine dry bread crumbs	1 tbsp.	15 mL
Water	1 tbsp.	15 mL
Ground cinnamon	1/2 tsp.	2 mL
Ground allspice	1/8 tsp.	0.5 mL
Ground cumin	1/8 tsp.	0.5 mL
Salt	1/4 tsp.	1 mL
Pepper, sprinkle		
Lean ground lamb	1/2 lb.	225 g
Cooking oil	1 tsp.	5 mL
Apple jelly	2 tbsp.	30 mL
Water	1 tbsp.	15 mL
Cayenne pepper, sprinkle		

Combine first 9 ingredients in small bowl. Add lamb. Mix well. Roll into twelve 1 inch (2.5 cm) balls.

Heat cooking oil in small frying pan on medium. Add meatballs. Cook for about 5 minutes, stirring occasionally, until browned on all sides. Reduce heat to low. Cook, covered, for about 5 minutes until no longer pink inside and internal temperature reaches 160°F (71°C). Drain.

Combine remaining 3 ingredients in small bowl. Add to meatballs. Stir until coated. Serves 2.

1 serving: 414 Calories; 24.9 g Total Fat (10.9 g Mono, 2.3 g Poly, 9.4 g Sat); 110 mg Cholesterol; 18 g Carbohydrate; trace Fibre; 29 g Protein; 418 mg Sodium

Spicy Pork And Bulgur

Fluffy bulgur is the perfect accompaniment for spicy pork and sweet peppers.

Pineapple juice	3/4 cup	175 mL
Bulgur	1/2 cup	125 mL
Cooking oil	1 tsp.	5 mL
Pork tenderloin, trimmed of fat and diced	1/2 lb.	225 g
Chopped onion	1/2 cup	125 mL
Small garlic clove, minced	1	1
(or 1/8 tsp., 0.5 mL, powder)		
Diced red pepper	1 cup	250 mL
Red jalapeño jelly	1 tbsp.	15 mL
Dried crushed chilies	1/4 tsp.	1 mL
Salt	1/2 tsp.	2 mL
Pepper	1/8 tsp.	0.5 mL

Measure pineapple juice into small saucepan. Bring to a boil. Add bulgur. Stir. Remove from heat. Let stand, covered, for about 30 minutes until liquid is absorbed and bulgur is tender.

Heat cooking oil in medium frying pan on medium-high. Add next 3 ingredients. Cook for 5 to 8 minutes, stirring often, until pork is no longer pink inside. Reduce heat to medium.

Add remaining 5 ingredients. Cook for about 2 minutes, stirring occasionally, until red pepper is tender-crisp. Add bulgur. Stir. Makes about 3 cups (750 mL). Serves 2.

1 serving: 394 Calories; 7.8 g Total Fat (3.6 g Mono, 1.5 g Poly, 2.0 g Sat); 71 mg Cholesterol; 54 g Carbohydrate; 6 g Fibre; 29 g Protein; 653 mg Sodium

Pictured on page 90.

Paré Pointer

He hammers like lightning—he seldom hits the same place twice.

Sausage And Lentils

Healthy lentils never tasted better! Pairing them with smoky sausage makes the perfect dinner for a cold winter's day. Serve with a green salad for a complete meal.

Cooking oil	1/2 tsp.	2 mL
Smoked ham sausage, cut into 1/2 inch (12 mm) slices	1/2 lb.	225 g
Finely chopped carrot	1/4 cup	60 mL
Finely chopped celery	1/4 cup	60 mL
Finely chopped onion	1/4 cup	60 mL
Garlic cloves, minced (or 1/2 tsp., 2 mL powder)	2	2
Seasoned salt	1/2 tsp.	2 mL
Can of lentils, rinsed and drained	19 oz.	540 mL
Frozen peas	1/2 cup	125 mL
Chopped tomato	1/4 cup	60 mL
Chopped fresh thyme (or sprinkle of dried)	1/4 tsp.	1 mL

Heat cooking oil in large frying pan on medium. Add sausage. Cook for about 3 minutes, stirring occasionally, until browned.

Add next 5 ingredients. Cook for about 3 minutes, stirring often, until onion is softened.

Add lentils and peas. Heat and stir until heated through.

Add tomato and thyme. Stir. Makes about 2 1/2 cups (625 mL). Serves 2.

1 serving: 482 Calories; 14.5 g Total Fat (0.7 g Mono, 0.5 g Poly, 0.1 g Sat); 0 mg Cholesterol; 50 g Carbohydrate; 22 g Fibre; 38 g Protein; 1802 mg Sodium

Pictured on page 90.

Pictured on page 90.

Paprika Mushroom Pork

Reminiscent of stroganoff, this savoury combination of pork, mushrooms and sour cream is best served over egg noodles to soak up all the tasty sauce.

All-purpose flour	1 tbsp.	15 mL
Salt	1/8 tsp.	0.5 mL
Boneless pork sirloin steak, cut into 1/4 inch (3 mm) slices (see Tip, page 93)	1/2 lb.	225 g
Cooking oil	2 tsp.	10 mL
Cooking oil	1 tsp.	5 mL
Sliced fresh white mushrooms	1 cup	250 mL
Chopped onion	1/2 cup	125 mL
Paprika	1 tsp.	5 mL
Prepared chicken broth	2/3 cup	150 mL
Sour cream	1/4 cup	60 mL
Chopped fresh dill (or 3/4 tsp., 4 mL, dried)	1 tbsp.	15 mL

Combine flour and salt in large resealable freezer bag. Add pork. Seal bag. Toss until coated.

Heat first amount of cooking oil in medium frying pan on medium-high. Add pork. Cook for 3 to 5 minutes, stirring often, until browned. Remove to plate. Cover to keep warm. Reduce heat to medium.

Heat second amount of cooking oil in same frying pan. Add next 3 ingredients. Cook for about 5 minutes, stirring occasionally, until onion starts to brown.

Add broth. Stir. Bring to a boil. Add sour cream, dill and pork. Heat and stir for 1 to 2 minutes until pork is no longer pink inside and sauce is heated through. Makes about 2 cups (500 mL). Serves 2.

1 serving: 323 Calories; 19.1 g Total Fat (8.6 g Mono, 3.1 g Poly, 6.1 g Sat); 84 mg Cholesterol; 10 g Carbohydrate; 1 g Fibre; 27 g Protein; 716 mg Sodium

Braised Spareribs

What's the best part of this recipe? Either it's the sweet and tangy sauce, or the meat that's so tender it's falling off the bones—you decide!

Pork side ribs, trimmed of fat and cut into 2-bone portions	1 1/2 lbs.	680 g
Butter (or hard margarine)	2 tsp.	10 mL
Chopped onion	1/2 cup	125 mL
Ketchup	1/4 cup	60 mL
Brown sugar, packed	2 tbsp.	30 mL
Orange juice	2 tbsp.	30 mL
White vinegar	2 tbsp.	30 mL
Worcestershire sauce	1 tsp.	5 mL
Prepared mustard	1/2 tsp.	2 mL

Arrange ribs, meat-side up, in ungreased 1 1/2 quart (1.5 L) casserole.

Melt butter in medium saucepan on medium. Add onion. Cook for about 5 minutes, stirring often, until softened.

Add remaining 6 ingredients. Stir. Spoon over ribs. Bake, covered, in 325°F (160°C) oven for about 2 hours until ribs are very tender. Serves 2.

1 serving: 746 Calories; 53.8 g Total Fat (22.6 g Mono, 4.8 g Poly, 21.3 g Sat); 175 mg Cholesterol; 27 g Carbohydrate; 1 g Fibre; 37 g Protein; 594 mg Sodium

1. Herbed Scones, page 137
2. Roasted Balsamic Vegetables, page 114
3. Mediterranean Rack Of Lamb, page 94

Props courtesy of: Stokes

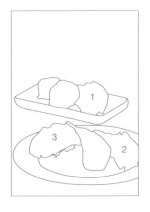

Chili Tomato Chops

Cumin and chili powder kick up the flavour of these tender pork chops.

Cooking oil	2 tsp.	10 mL
Bone-in pork chops (about 3/4 inch, 2 cm, thick), trimmed of fat	2	2
Chili powder	1/4 tsp.	1 mL
Salt	1/4 tsp.	1 mL
Pepper	1/4 tsp.	1 mL
Chopped Roma (plum) tomato	1 cup	250 mL
Lime juice	1 tbsp.	15 mL
Liquid honey	1 tbsp.	15 mL
Chili powder	1 tsp.	5 mL
Dried oregano	1/2 tsp.	2 mL
Ground cumin	1/4 tsp.	1 mL

Heat cooking oil in medium frying pan on medium. Add pork. Sprinkle with next 3 ingredients. Cook for about 5 minutes per side until browned.

Add remaining 6 ingredients. Stir. Reduce heat to medium-low. Cook, covered, for about 5 minutes until pork is no longer pink inside. Serves 2.

1 serving: 233 Calories; 10.3 g Total Fat (5.1 g Mono, 2.2 g Poly, 2.2 g Sat); 47 mg Cholesterol; 15 g Carbohydrate; 2 g Fibre; 20 g Protein; 354 mg Sodium

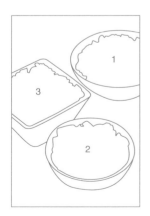

1. Spicy Pork And Bulgur, page 85
2. Pork And Almond Stir-Fry, page 92
3. Sausage And Lentils, page 86

Props courtesy of: Stokes

Pork And Almond Stir-Fry

Although this isn't an overly saucy stir-fry, there's certainly no shortage of flavour. Serve over jasmine rice or egg noodles.

Garlic powder	1/2 tsp.	2 mL
Ground ginger	1/2 tsp.	2 mL
Pepper	1/4 tsp.	1 mL
Boneless centre-cut pork chops, cut into 1/4 inch (6 mm) slices (see Tip, page 93)	2	2
Oyster sauce	1 tbsp.	15 mL
Chili paste (sambal oelek)	1 tsp.	5 mL
Soy sauce	1 tsp.	5 mL
Sesame oil (for flavour)	1 tsp.	5 mL
Sesame oil (for flavour)	1 tsp.	5 mL
Fresh asparagus, trimmed of tough ends and cut into 1 inch (2.5 cm) pieces	1/2 cup	125 mL
Snow peas, trimmed and cut in half	1/2 cup	125 mL
Slivered almonds, toasted (see Tip, page 103)	1/4 cup	1 mL

Combine first 3 ingredients in small bowl. Add pork. Toss until coated.

Combine next 3 ingredients in small cup. Set aside.

Heat medium frying pan on medium-high until very hot. Add first amount of sesame oil. Add pork. Stir-fry for about 1 minute until no longer pink. Remove to small bowl.

Add second amount of sesame oil to same frying pan. Add asparagus and snow peas. Stir-fry for about 1 minute until tender-crisp. Add almonds, pork and oyster sauce mixture. Heat and stir for about 1 minute until heated through. Makes about 1 1/2 cups (375 mL). Serves 2.

1 serving: 330 Calories; 19.5 g Total Fat (10.2 g Mono, 4.5 g Poly, 3.5 g Sat); 61 mg Cholesterol; 10 g Carbohydrate; 4 g Fibre; 29 g Protein; 290 mg Sodium

Pictured on page 90.

Lamb Chops With Thai Pesto

Thai pesto? Seems unusual, but this unique combination makes a great partner for tender lamb chops.

Lamb loin chops	1 lb.	454 g
Seasoned salt	1/4 tsp.	1 mL
THAI PESTO		
Coarsely chopped fresh cilantro	1/4 cup	60 mL
Salted cashews	1/4 cup	60 mL
Lime juice	2 tbsp.	30 mL
Medium sweetened coconut	2 tbsp.	30 mL
Olive oil	2 tbsp.	30 mL
Water	2 tsp.	10 mL
Sweet chili sauce	1 1/2 tsp.	7 mL
Coconut extract	1/8 tsp.	0.5 mL
Lime wedges, for garnish		

Sprinkle lamb with seasoned salt. Place on greased broiler pan. Broil for about 3 minutes per side or until lamb reaches desired doneness. Cover with foil. Let stand for 5 minutes.

Thai Pesto: Process first 8 ingredients in blender or food processor until almost smooth. Makes about 1/3 cup (75 mL) pesto. Serve with lamb.

Garnish with lime wedges. Serves 2.

1 serving: 694 Calories; 56.3 g Total Fat (22.8 g Mono, 4.2 g Poly, 18.7 g Sat); 131 mg Cholesterol; 10 g Carbohydrate; 1 g Fibre; 37 g Protein; 454 mg Sodium

 tip To slice meat easily, freeze for about 30 minutes until just starting to freeze. If using from frozen state, partially thaw before cutting.

Mediterranean Rack Of Lamb

The perfect solution for a romantic dinner for two. The best part of this impressive dish is that you won't have to slave over the stove all day. Comes with a flavourful side of minted couscous built right into the recipe.

Cooking oil	1 tsp.	5 mL
Rack of lamb (see Note 1)	1 lb.	454 g
Salt, sprinkle		
Pepper, sprinkle		
Mint jelly	2 tbsp.	30 mL
MINTED COUSCOUS		
Olive (or cooking) oil	2 tsp.	10 mL
Finely chopped onion	1/4 cup	60 mL
Pine nuts	2 tbsp.	30 mL
Prepared chicken broth	1/2 cup	125 mL
Couscous	1/2 cup	125 mL
Finely chopped tomato	1/4 cup	60 mL
Crumbled feta cheese	3 tbsp.	50 mL
Chopped fresh mint	2 tsp.	10 mL
(or 1/2 tsp., 2 mL, dried), see Note 2		
Chopped fresh oregano	1 tsp.	5 mL
(or 1/4 tsp., 1 mL, dried), see Note 2		

Heat cooking oil in large frying pan on medium-high. Sprinkle lamb with salt and pepper. Add to pan, meat-side down. Cook for about 3 minutes until browned. Place, meat-side up, on greased baking sheet.

Put mint jelly into small microwave-safe bowl. Microwave on high (100%) for about 30 seconds until melted. Brush over lamb. Cook in 375°F (190°C) oven for about 16 minutes until meat thermometer inserted into thickest part of lamb reads 135°F (57°C) for medium-rare or until desired doneness. Cover with foil. Let stand for 10 minutes. Cut into 2-bone portions.

Minted Couscous: Heat olive oil in small saucepan on medium. Add onion and pine nuts. Cook for about 6 minutes, stirring often, until pine nuts are toasted and onion is browned.

(continued on next page)

Pork & Lamb

Add broth. Stir. Bring to a boil. Add couscous. Stir. Remove from heat. Let stand, covered, for about 5 minutes until liquid is absorbed. Fluff with fork.

Add remaining 4 ingredients. Stir. Makes about 1 1/2 cups (375 mL) couscous. Transfer to serving plate. Arrange lamb over top. Serves 2.

1 serving: 874 Calories; 56.2 g Total Fat (23.8 g Mono, 5.2 g Poly, 23.9 g Sat); 127 mg Cholesterol; 51 g Carbohydrate; 4 g Fibre; 39 g Protein; 661 mg Sodium

Pictured on page 89.

Note 1: Fresh racks of lamb are available in single-rack portions with an average weight of about 1 lb. (454 g). You could also use a thawed frozen lamb rack, but these are usually smaller so the cooking time should be reduced.

Note 2: If you are using dried herbs instead of fresh, add them with the couscous and broth rather than at the end.

Balsamic Tea-Glazed Chops

Now you can enjoy the flavours of one of your favourite drinks in a tangy pork chop! Iced tea makes for a unique and fun addition to these saucy chops.

Olive (or cooking) oil	1 tsp.	5 mL
Boneless pork loin chops, trimmed of fat	2	2
(about 3/4 inch, 2 cm, thick)		
Salt, sprinkle		
Pepper, sprinkle		
Balsamic vinegar	1/3 cup	75 mL
Prepared iced tea	1/3 cup	75 mL

Heat olive oil in medium frying pan on medium-high. Add pork. Sprinkle with salt and pepper. Cook for about 3 minutes per side until browned. Reduce heat to medium-low.

Add vinegar and iced tea. Cook, uncovered, for 2 to 3 minutes per side until pork is no longer pink inside. Remove pork to plate. Cover to keep warm. Increase heat to medium. Boil gently for about 5 minutes until liquid is slightly reduced. Serve with pork. Serves 2.

1 serving: 211 Calories; 8.3 g Total Fat (4.4 g Mono, 0.6 g Poly, 2.5 g Sat); 61 mg Cholesterol; 9 g Carbohydrate; 0 g Fibre; 22 g Protein; 58 mg Sodium

Vegetable Ricotta Loaf

A flavourful vegetable layer tops a smooth lemon-scented base of ricotta cheese. Serve with a drizzle of balsamic vinaigrette.

Cooking oil	1 tsp.	5 mL
Chopped fresh white mushrooms	2 cups	500 mL
Chopped onion	1/2 cup	125 mL
Chopped red pepper	1/2 cup	125 mL
Italian seasoning	3/4 tsp.	4 mL
Salt	1/2 tsp.	2 mL
Large egg, fork-beaten	1	1
Ricotta cheese	1/2 cup	125 mL
Cornstarch	1 tbsp.	15 mL
Grated lemon zest	1/2 tsp.	2 mL

Heat cooking oil in medium frying pan on medium. Add mushrooms and onion. Cook for about 15 minutes, stirring often, until mushrooms are browned and liquid has evaporated.

Add next 3 ingredients. Cook for about 3 minutes, stirring occasionally, until red pepper is tender-crisp. Spread in greased 2 cup (500 mL) casserole.

Whisk remaining 4 ingredients in small bowl until smooth. Pour over vegetables. Bake in 400°F (205°C) oven for about 20 minutes until lightly browned on edges and knife inserted in centre comes out clean. Let stand for 5 minutes. Run knife along inside edge of casserole. Invert onto serving plate. Serves 2.

1 serving: 198 Calories; 9.9 g Total Fat (3.8 g Mono, 1.3 g Poly, 4.0 g Sat); 112 mg Cholesterol; 16 g Carbohydrate; 1 g Fibre; 12 g Protein; 699 mg Sodium

Tortellini And Vegetables

Cheese tortellini and fresh vegetables are tossed in a tangy mustard sauce for a very filling vegetarian meal.

Water	8 cups	2 L
Salt	1 tsp.	5 mL
Fresh cheese-filled tortellini	2 cups	500 mL
Broccoli florets	1 cup	250 mL
Snow peas, trimmed and halved	1 cup	250 mL
Thinly sliced carrot	1/2 cup	125 mL
Prepared vegetable broth	3/4 cup	175 mL
Cornstarch	1 tsp.	5 mL
Dijon mustard (with whole seeds)	2 tbsp.	30 mL
Chopped tomato	3/4 cup	175 mL
Sour cream	1/3 cup	75 mL
Sliced green onion	2 tbsp.	30 mL

Combine water and salt in large saucepan or Dutch oven. Bring to a boil. Add tortellini. Boil, uncovered, for 6 minutes, stirring occasionally.

Add next 3 ingredients. Cook for about 2 minutes, stirring occasionally, until tortellini is tender but firm and vegetables are tender-crisp. Drain. Return to same pot. Cover to keep warm.

Stir broth into cornstarch in small saucepan. Add mustard. Heat and stir on medium until boiling and thickened.

Add remaining 3 ingredients. Add to tortellini mixture. Stir. Makes about 5 cups (1.25 L). Serves 2.

1 serving: 495 Calories; 18.7 g Total Fat (2.1 g Mono, 0.5 g Poly, 8.9 g Sat); 41 mg Cholesterol; 63 g Carbohydrate; 7 g Fibre; 21 g Protein; 946 mg Sodium

Pictured on page 107.

Spicy Bean Bowl

Everyone knows that beans are good for you, but isn't there some way to make this healthy ingredient a little more exciting? We've spiced them up for a bowl of hearty goodness with some serious sass!

Cooking oil	1 tsp.	5 mL
Chopped onion	1/2 cup	125 mL
Small garlic clove, minced	1	1
(or 1/8 tsp., 0.5 mL, powder)		
Chili powder	1/2 tsp.	2 mL
Can of pinto beans, rinsed and drained	14 oz.	398 mL
Tomato sauce	1 cup	250 mL
Diced yellow pepper	1/2 cup	125 mL
Grated carrot	1/2 cup	125 mL
Chopped pickled jalapeño pepper	1 tsp.	5 mL
Salt	1/8 tsp.	0.5 mL
Pepper	1/8 tsp.	0.5 mL

Heat cooking oil in large frying pan on medium. Add next 3 ingredients. Cook for about 3 minutes, stirring often, until onion is softened.

Add remaining 7 ingredients. Cook, covered, for 10 minutes, stirring occasionally, to blend flavours. Makes about 2 cups (500 mL). Serves 2.

1 serving: 269 Calories; 4.3 g Total Fat (1.4 g Mono, 2.4 g Poly, 0.2 g Sat); 0 mg Cholesterol; 47 g Carbohydrate; 14 g Fibre; 14 g Protein; 1317 mg Sodium

Hot Tamale Enchiladas

This recipe provides a tasty shortcut for making hot tamales—corn tortillas!
Packed with all the spicy flavours you'd expect.

Cooking oil	1/2 tsp.	2 mL
Chopped onion	1/2 cup	125 mL
Small garlic clove, minced	1	1
(or 1/8 tsp., 0.5 mL, powder)		
Ground cumin	1/2 tsp.	2 mL
Canned diced tomatoes, drained	1 cup	250 mL
Canned white kidney beans,	1 cup	250 mL
rinsed and drained		
Grated jalapeño Monterey Jack cheese	1 cup	250 mL
Chopped chipotle pepper in adobo sauce	1/2 tsp.	2 mL
(see Tip, page 40)		
Corn tortillas (6 inch, 15 cm, diameter)	4	4
Grated jalapeño Monterey Jack cheese	1/2 cup	125 mL

Heat cooking oil in small saucepan on medium. Add next 3 ingredients. Cook for about 3 minutes, stirring often, until onion is starting to soften.

Add next 4 ingredients. Stir.

Spoon bean mixture down centre of each tortilla. Roll to enclose filling. Place, seam-side down, in greased 1 quart (1 L) baking dish.

Sprinkle with second amount of cheese. Bake, uncovered, in 375°F (190°C) oven for about 15 minutes until cheese is melted and golden. Serves 2.

1 serving: 597 Calories; 31.3 g Total Fat (0.7 g Mono, 0.4 g Poly, 15.1 g Sat); 75 mg Cholesterol; 57 g Carbohydrate; 9 g Fibre; 28 g Protein; 978 mg Sodium

Blackened Tofu Cutlets

Think flavourful tofu isn't possible? This recipe will change your mind. Fiery Cajun spices and a crunchy cornmeal crust transform this nutritious soy product from blah to Mardi Gras!

All-purpose flour	2 tbsp.	30 mL
Large egg	1	1
Cajun seasoning	2 tbsp.	30 mL
Yellow cornmeal	2 tbsp.	30 mL
Package of extra-firm tofu (12 oz., 350 g)	1/2	1/2
Cooking oil	1 tbsp.	15 mL

Measure flour into small shallow dish. Beat egg in separate small shallow dish. Combine seasoning and cornmeal on large plate.

Cut tofu horizontally into four 1/4 inch (6 mm) thick slices. Pat dry. Press both sides of tofu slices into flour. Dip into egg. Press both sides of tofu into cornmeal mixture until coated. Discard any remaining flour, egg and cornmeal mixture.

Heat cooking oil in medium frying pan on medium-high until very hot. Add tofu. Cook for about 2 minutes per side until coating is blackened. Serve immediately. Makes 4 cutlets. Serves 2.

1 serving: 153 Calories; 9.7 g Total Fat (4.9 g Mono, 3.1 g Poly, 1.1 g Sat); 47 mg Cholesterol; 8 g Carbohydrate; trace Fibre; 9 g Protein; 879 mg Sodium

---

Paré Pointer

The ghost couldn't go to the party because he had no-body to go with.

Vegetarian

Greek Angel Pasta

All your favourite Greek flavours together in one tasty combination of pasta, vegetables, tapenade and feta.

Water	12 cups	3 L
Salt	1 1/2 tsp.	7 mL
Angel hair pasta	7 oz.	200 g
Olive (or cooking) oil	1 tsp.	5 mL
Chopped red pepper	1/2 cup	125 mL
Chopped yellow pepper	1/2 cup	125 mL
Can of diced tomatoes (with juice)	14 oz.	398 mL
Pepper	1/4 tsp.	1 mL
Crumbled feta cheese	1/2 cup	125 mL
Sliced green onion	1/4 cup	60 mL
Black olive tapenade	2 tbsp.	30 mL
Chopped fresh basil	1 tbsp.	15 mL

Combine water and salt in Dutch oven. Bring to a boil. Add pasta. Boil, uncovered, for 3 to 5 minutes, stirring occasionally, until tender but firm. Drain. Return to same pot. Cover to keep warm.

Heat olive oil in large frying pan on medium-high. Add red and yellow peppers. Cook for about 2 minutes, stirring occasionally, until peppers start to brown.

Add tomatoes and pepper. Reduce heat to medium-low. Simmer, uncovered, for about 5 minutes until reduced by half and peppers are softened.

Add remaining 4 ingredients and pasta. Toss until coated. Makes about 5 1/2 cups (1.4 L). Serves 2.

1 serving: 583 Calories; 14.3 g Total Fat (3.5 g Mono, 0.5 g Poly, 6.4 g Sat); 36 mg Cholesterol; 91 g Carbohydrate; 3 g Fibre; 21 g Protein; 1077 mg Sodium

Pictured on page 107.

Tahini Lentil Loaf

Tahini, also known as sesame paste, is a common ingredient in Middle Eastern cooking. It can also be used as an ingredient in hummus or as a sandwich spread. Here, it adds great flavour to a hearty lentil loaf.

Olive (or cooking) oil	1/2 tsp.	2 mL
Finely chopped celery	1/4 cup	60 mL
Finely chopped onion	1/4 cup	60 mL
Small garlic clove, minced	1	1
(or 1/8 tsp., 0.5 mL, powder)		
Ground cumin	1/2 tsp.	2 mL
Dried oregano	1/4 tsp.	1 mL
Salt	1/4 tsp.	1 mL
Pepper	1/4 tsp.	1 mL
Canned lentils, rinsed and drained	1 1/2 cups	375 mL
Finely chopped red pepper	1/4 cup	60 mL
Finely chopped walnuts, toasted	1/4 cup	60 mL
(see Tip, page 103)		
Tahini (sesame paste)	3 tbsp.	50 mL
Fine dry bread crumbs	2 tbsp.	30 mL
Olive (or cooking) oil	1 tsp.	5 mL
Sesame seeds, toasted	2 tsp.	10 mL
(see Tip, page 103)		

Heat first amount of olive oil in medium frying pan on medium. Add next 7 ingredients. Cook for about 10 minutes, stirring occasionally, until vegetables are softened.

Add lentils. Heat and stir for 5 minutes. Transfer to small bowl.

Add next 4 ingredients. Stir. Shape into loaf in greased 9 inch (22 cm) pie plate.

Brush with second amount of olive oil. Sprinkle with sesame seeds. Bake in 375°F (190°C) oven for about 20 minutes until heated through. Serve immediately. Serves 2.

1 serving: 486 Calories; 27.4 g Total Fat (9.2 g Mono, 13.5 g Poly, 3.4 g Sat); 0 mg Cholesterol; 44 g Carbohydrate; 17 g Fibre; 21 g Protein; 593 mg Sodium

Curry Chickpea Bake

Curry and chickpeas are a natural pair. Baking them together in a convenient casserole just makes this combination that much easier to enjoy.

Can of chickpeas (garbanzo beans), rinsed and drained	19 oz.	540 mL
Arborio rice	1/2 cup	125 mL
Cooking oil	1 tsp.	5 mL
Chopped onion	1/2 cup	125 mL
Hot curry paste	1 tbsp.	15 mL
Small garlic clove, minced (or 1/8 tsp., 1 mL, powder)	1	1
Coconut milk (or reconstituted from powder)	1 cup	250 mL
Prepared vegetable broth	1/2 cup	125 mL
Liquid honey	1 tsp.	5 mL
Salt	1/4 tsp.	1 mL
Chopped fresh parsley	1 tsp.	5 mL

Combine chickpeas and rice in greased 2 quart (2 L) casserole. Set aside.

Heat cooking oil in small saucepan on medium. Add next 3 ingredients. Cook for about 5 minutes, stirring often, until onion is softened.

Add next 4 ingredients. Stir. Bring to a boil. Pour over chickpea mixture. Stir. Bake, covered, in 400°F (205°C) oven for about 35 minutes until rice is tender and liquid is almost absorbed. Let stand, covered, for about 5 minutes until liquid is absorbed.

Sprinkle with parsley. Makes about 3 1/2 cups (875 mL).

1 cup (250 mL): 356 Calories; 19.2 g Total Fat (2.0 g Mono, 1.7 g Poly, 13.3 g Sat); 0 mg Cholesterol; 39 g Carbohydrate; 7 g Fibre; 10 g Protein; 559 mg Sodium

 tip
When toasting nuts, seeds or coconut, cooking times will vary for each type of nut—so never toast them together. For small amounts, place ingredient in an ungreased frying pan. Heat on medium for 3 to 5 minutes, stirring often, until golden. For larger amounts, spread ingredient evenly in an ungreased shallow pan. Bake in a 350°F (175°C) oven for 5 to 10 minutes, stirring or shaking often, until golden.

Vegetarian

Italian Quesadillas

You may just have super strength after eating one of these quesadillas—they're packed with plenty of spinach! Veggie ground round adds a dose of protein.

Fresh spinach leaves, lightly packed	4 cups	1 L
Water	2 tbsp.	30 mL
Sun-dried tomato pesto	1 tsp.	5 mL
Grated Italian cheese blend	1 cup	250 mL
Sun-dried tomato (or plain) flour tortillas (9 inch, 22 cm, diameter)	2	2
Italian veggie ground round (see Note), crumbled	1/2 cup	125 mL

Cooking spray

Combine spinach and water in medium microwave-safe bowl. Microwave, covered, on high (100%) for about 2 minutes until just wilted. Let stand for about 5 minutes until cool enough to handle. Drain. Squeeze dry. Add pesto. Stir. Set aside.

Sprinkle 1/4 cup (60 mL) cheese over half of each tortilla. Scatter spinach over cheese. Sprinkle ground round over spinach. Top with remaining cheese. Fold tortillas in half to cover filling. Press down lightly. Arrange on greased baking sheet.

Spray quesadillas with cooking spray. Bake in 425°F (220°C) oven for about 10 minutes until cheese is melted and edges start to brown. Cut quesadillas in half. Makes 4 wedges. Serves 2.

1 serving: 296 Calories; 7.8 g Total Fat (trace Mono, 0.1 g Poly, 3.0 g Sat); 10 mg Cholesterol; 29 g Carbohydrate; 4 g Fibre; 28 g Protein; 1008 mg Sodium

Note: Veggie ground round is available in the produce section of your grocery store.

Southwestern Spaghetti Squash

Enjoy the bright, cheery colours and hearty flavours of this quick one-dish meal. Serve on its own or over rice for hungrier folk.

Spaghetti squash	1 lb.	454 g
Water	3 tbsp.	50 mL
Cooking oil	2 tsp.	10 mL
Chopped onion	1/4 cup	60 mL
Small garlic clove, minced	1	1
(or 1/8 tsp., 0.5 mL, powder)		
Chili powder	1/4 tsp.	1 mL
Ground cumin	1/4 tsp.	1 mL
Canned black beans, rinsed and drained	1 cup	250 mL
Chopped red pepper	1/2 cup	125 mL
Chopped Roma (plum) tomato	1/2 cup	125 mL
Frozen kernel corn	1/2 cup	125 mL
Lime juice	1 tbsp.	15 mL
Grated lime zest	1 tsp.	5 mL
Finely chopped chipotle pepper in	1 tsp.	5 mL
adobo sauce (see Tip, page 40)		
Salt	1/2 tsp.	2 mL
Grated Monterey Jack cheese	1/3 cup	75 mL
Chopped fresh cilantro or parsley,		
for garnish		

Cut squash in half lengthwise. Using spoon, scoop out and discard seeds. Place, cut-side down, in 2 quart (2 L) casserole. Add water. Microwave, covered, on high (100%) for about 10 minutes until tender. Drain. Let stand, covered, for 5 minutes. Separate into strands using fork. Transfer to small bowl. Discard shells.

Heat cooking oil in large frying pan on medium. Add next 4 ingredients. Cook for about 5 minutes, stirring often, until onion is softened.

Add next 8 ingredients and squash. Stir well. Cook, covered, for about 5 minutes until heated through. Spoon onto 2 serving plates.

Sprinkle with cheese. Garnish with cilantro. Serves 2.

1 serving: 265 Calories; 10.7 g Total Fat (2.7 g Mono, 1.6 g Poly, 3.8 g Sat); 17 mg Cholesterol; 37 g Carbohydrate; 10 g Fibre; 12 g Protein; 1266 mg Sodium

Pictured on page 107.

Vegetarian

Pear And Spinach Casserole

*Pear may not be an ingredient you'd expect to see in a casserole,
but this recipe combines this juicy fruit with the classic flavours of blue
cheese and spinach to create some classy comfort food.*

Large eggs	2	2
Milk	3/4 cup	175 mL
All-purpose flour	1/2 cup	125 mL
Baking powder	1/2 tsp.	2 mL
Salt	1/4 tsp.	1 mL
Pepper	1/8 tsp.	0.5 mL
Chopped peeled firm pear	1 1/4 cups	300 mL
Chopped fresh spinach leaves, lightly packed	1 cup	250 mL
Crumbled blue cheese (about 1 1/8 oz., 32 g)	3 tbsp.	50 mL
Grated havarti cheese (about 1 oz., 28 g)	3 tbsp.	50 mL

Whisk first 6 ingredients in medium bowl until smooth.

Add remaining 4 ingredients. Stir. Transfer to greased 1 quart (1 L)
casserole. Bake in 400°F (205°C) oven for about 35 minutes until knife
inserted in centre comes out clean. Let stand for 5 minutes. Serves 2.

*1 serving: 406 Calories; 16.6 g Total Fat (2.5 g Mono, 0.8 g Poly, 9.2 g Sat); 220 mg Cholesterol;
44 g Carbohydrate; 4 g Fibre; 19 g Protein; 735 mg Sodium*

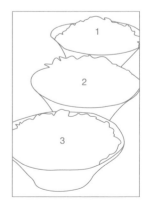

Vegetarian

Honey Ginger Vegetables

Sweet or spicy? These tender-crisp veggies are both! Honey lends some mild sweetness, while ginger gives a touch of heat. A simple microwave method gets this tasty side on the table in no time.

Water	1/4 cup	60 mL
Liquid honey	1 tbsp.	15 mL
Finely grated ginger root	1 tsp.	5 mL
(or 1/4 tsp., 1 mL, ground ginger)		
Sesame oil (for flavour)	1/2 tsp.	2 mL
Salt	1/4 tsp.	1 mL
Pepper	1/8 tsp.	0.5 mL
Frozen Oriental mixed vegetables	2 cups	500 mL

Combine first 6 ingredients in medium microwave-safe dish. Add vegetables. Toss. Microwave, covered, on high (100%) for about 5 minutes, stirring twice, until tender-crisp. Toss until coated. Drain any remaining liquid. Makes about 1 1/4 cups (300 mL). Serves 2.

1 serving: 127 Calories; 2.6 g Total Fat (0.4 g Mono, 0.5 g Poly, 0.5 g Sat); trace Cholesterol; 22 g Carbohydrate; 1 g Fibre; 3 g Protein; 854 mg Sodium

Pictured at left.

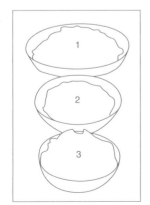

1. Sweet Potato And Apple Mash, page 121
2. Shiitake Risotto, page 119
3. Honey Ginger Vegetables, above

Props courtesy of: Danesco Inc.

Citrus Veggie Pasta

Perk things up at your dinner table with this pasta tossed with sunny citrus and a little peppery pizzaz! The perfect dinner companion for chicken or pork.

Water	4 cups	1 L
Salt	1/2 tsp.	2 mL
Rotini pasta	2/3 cup	150 mL
Olive (or cooking) oil	1/2 tsp.	2 mL
Chopped onion	1/2 cup	125 mL
Garlic clove, minced	1	1
(or 1/4 tsp., 1 mL, powder)		
Finely chopped red pepper	1/4 cup	60 mL
Frozen cut green beans, thawed	1/4 cup	60 mL
Olive oil	2 tsp.	10 mL
Grated lemon zest	1/4 tsp.	1 mL
Grated orange zest	1/4 tsp.	1 mL
Salt	1/4 tsp.	1 mL
Pepper	1/4 tsp.	1 mL
Grated Parmesan cheese	2 tbsp.	30 mL

Combine water and salt in large saucepan. Bring to a boil. Add pasta. Boil, uncovered, for about 12 to 14 minutes, stirring occasionally, until pasta is tender but firm. Drain. Return to same pot. Cover to keep warm.

Heat olive oil in medium frying pan on medium. Add onion and garlic. Cook for about 5 minutes, stirring often, until onion is softened.

Add red pepper and green beans. Cook for about 3 minutes until red pepper is tender-crisp. Add to pasta. Toss.

Add next 5 ingredients. Toss.

Sprinkle with cheese. Makes about 1 1/2 cups (375 mL). Serves 2.

1 serving: 185 Calories; 7.9 g Total Fat (4.7 g Mono, 0.6 g Poly, 2.1 g Sat); 5 mg Cholesterol; 23 g Carbohydrate; 2 g Fibre; 6 g Protein; 412 mg Sodium

Mushroom Lasagna

Lasagna's not just for dinner anymore—this light version makes a great side for chicken or pork. Serve with baguette slices to soak up the delicious sauce.

Water	8 cups	2 L
Salt	1 tsp.	5 mL
Lasagna noodles	4	4
Butter (or hard margarine)	2 tsp.	10 mL
Cooking oil	2 tsp.	10 mL
Sliced fresh white mushrooms	2 cups	500 mL
Finely chopped onion	1/4 cup	60 mL
Garlic clove, minced	1	1
(or 1/4 tsp., 1 mL, powder)		
Salt	1/4 tsp.	1 mL
Dry (or alcohol-free) white wine	1/3 cup	75 mL
Grated Italian cheese blend	1/3 cup	75 mL
Chopped fresh parsley, for garnish		

Combine water and salt in large saucepan or Dutch oven. Bring to a boil. Add noodles. Boil, uncovered, for 12 to 15 minutes, stirring occasionally, until tender but firm. Drain. Cut noodles in half crosswise. Return to same pot. Cover to keep warm.

Heat butter and cooking oil in medium frying pan on medium. Add next 4 ingredients. Cook for about 5 minutes, stirring occasionally, until onion and mushrooms are softened.

Add wine. Bring to a boil. Cook for 2 minutes.

Layer mushroom mixture, noodles and cheese on 2 small plates, beginning and ending with mushroom mixture.

Garnish with parsley. Serve immediately. Serves 2.

1 serving: 347 Calories; 13.7 g Total Fat (3.7 g Mono, 1.5 g Poly, 5.9 g Sat); 23 mg Cholesterol; 38 g Carbohydrate; 2 g Fibre; 12 g Protein; 442 mg Sodium

Broccoli Sesame

Wonderful flavour and virtually hassle-free—no one will turn down a serving of healthy greens when they're served this way!

Broccoli florets	2 cups	500 mL
Water	1 tbsp.	15 mL
Butter (or hard margarine)	2 tsp.	10 mL
Sesame seeds, toasted (see Tip, page 103)	1 1/2 tsp.	7 mL
Soy sauce	1 1/2 tsp.	7 mL
Brown sugar, packed	1 tsp.	5 mL
White vinegar	1 tsp.	5 mL
Sesame oil (for flavour)	1/2 tsp.	2 mL

Put broccoli into medium microwave-safe bowl. Add water. Microwave, covered, on high (100%) for about 3 minutes until tender. Drain.

Combine remaining 6 ingredients in small microwave-safe cup. Microwave on high (100%) for about 1 minute until hot. Drizzle over broccoli. Toss gently. Makes about 2 cups (500 mL). Serves 2.

1 serving: 87 Calories; 6.3 g Total Fat (1.9 g Mono, 1.2 g Poly, 2.8 g Sat); 10 mg Cholesterol; 7 g Carbohydrate; 2 g Fibre; 3 g Protein; 245 mg Sodium

Autumn Squash With Apple Stuffing

This is the perfect accompaniment to a special autumn dinner for two!

Acorn squash	1 1/2 lbs	680 g
Chopped unpeeled cooking apple (such as McIntosh)	1 cup	250 mL
Chopped walnuts	1/4 cup	60 mL
Maple (or maple-flavoured) syrup	2 tbsp.	30 mL
Balsamic vinegar	2 tsp.	10 mL
Butter (or hard margarine), melted	1 tsp.	5 mL

(continued on next page)

Cut squash in half lengthwise. Using spoon, scoop out seeds and discard. Place squash halves, cut-side down, on ungreased baking sheet. Bake in 350°F (175°C) oven for 25 minutes.

Combine remaining 5 ingredients in small bowl. Spoon into squash halves. Bake for about 20 minutes until squash is tender. Cuts into 4 pieces.

1 piece: 169 Calories; 6.1 g Total Fat (0.9 g Mono, 3.7 g Poly, 1.1 g Sat); 3 mg Cholesterol; 30 g Carbohydrate; 4 g Fibre; 3 g Protein; 14 mg Sodium

Creamy Corn Gratin

This savoury dish gets a little natural sweetness from corn. No one would ever guess how simple this rich and creamy side is to prepare.

Frozen kernel corn, thawed	1 cup	250 mL
Whipping cream	1/4 cup	60 mL
Dried basil, just a pinch		
Dried thyme, just a pinch		
Salt, just a pinch		
Fine dry bread crumbs	1 tbsp.	15 mL
Grated Parmesan cheese	1 tbsp.	15 mL

Combine first 5 ingredients in small bowl. Transfer to greased 4 inch (10 cm) diameter round baking dish.

Combine bread crumbs and cheese in separate small bowl. Sprinkle over corn mixture. Bake in 350°F (175°C) oven for about 20 minutes until edges start to bubble. Turn on broiler. Broil for about 4 minutes until golden. Serves 2.

1 serving: 186 Calories; 11.9 g Total Fat (3.4 g Mono, 0.4 g Poly, 7.1 g Sat); 41 mg Cholesterol; 16 g Carbohydrate; 2 g Fibre; 4 g Protein; 102 mg Sodium

 tip To segment a citrus fruit, trim a small slice of peel from both ends so the flesh is exposed. Place the fruit, bottom cut-side down, on a cutting board. Remove the peel with a sharp knife, cutting down and around the flesh, leaving as little pith as possible. Over a small bowl, cut on either side of the membranes to release the segments.

Roasted Balsamic Vegetables

There's a double-dose of sweetness in this healthy vegetable side—balsamic vinegar adds tangy flavour while roasting the vegetables brings out their natural sugars.

Chopped portobello mushrooms (about 6 oz., 170 mL), about 1 inch (2.5 cm) pieces	2 cups	500 mL
Thinly sliced fennel bulb (white part only)	2 cups	500 mL
Chopped red pepper (1 inch, 2.5 cm, pieces)	1 cup	250 mL
Balsamic vinegar	2 tbsp.	30 mL
Olive (or cooking) oil	1 tbsp.	15 mL
Salt	1/2 tsp.	2 mL
Pepper	1/4 tsp.	1 mL

Toss all 7 ingredients in large bowl until coated. Arrange in single layer on greased baking sheet. Bake in 400°F (205°C) oven for about 30 minutes, stirring occasionally, until vegetables are browned and tender. Makes about 2 cups (500 mL). Serves 2.

1 serving: 227 Calories; 7.9 g Total Fat (5.0 g Mono, 0.8 g Poly, 1.0 g Sat); 0 mg Cholesterol; 38 g Carbohydrate; 15 g Fibre; 8 g Protein; 790 mg Sodium

Pictured on page 89.

Pesto Potatoes

The addition of a few simple ingredients makes ordinary mashed potatoes simply extraordinary! Sour cream adds a creamy texture and pesto adds lots of flavour.

Medium peeled potatoes, cut up	2	2
Milk	2 tbsp.	30 mL
Sour cream	2 tbsp.	30 mL
Sun-dried tomato pesto	1 tbsp.	15 mL
Salt	1/4 tsp.	1 mL
Pepper	1/8 tsp.	0.5 mL

(continued on next page)

114 Sides

Pour water into small saucepan until about 1 inch (2.5 cm) deep. Add potato. Cover. Bring to a boil. Reduce heat to medium. Boil gently for 12 to 15 minutes until tender. Drain. Mash.

Add remaining 5 ingredients. Mash until light and fluffy. Makes about 2 1/4 cups (550 mL). Serves 2.

1 serving: 182 Calories; 2.9 g Total Fat (0.8 g Mono, 0.2 g Poly, 1.8 g Sat); 7 mg Cholesterol; 36 g Carbohydrate; 3 g Fibre; 4 g Protein; 395 mg Sodium

Orange Mint Beets

The name says it all! Sweet roasted beets get a little help from tangy orange and fresh mint.

Fresh beets, scrubbed clean and trimmed (see Tip, below)	12 oz.	340 g
Small orange, segmented (see Tip, page 113)	1	1
Chopped fresh mint (or 1/4 tsp., 1 mL, dried)	1 tsp.	5 mL
Salt, just a pinch		

Wrap beets in foil. Bake in 350°F (175°C) oven for about 1 1/2 hours until tender. Unwrap. Let stand until cool enough to handle. Peel beets. Cut into 8 wedges each. Put into small bowl.

Add remaining 3 ingredients. Toss. Makes about 1 1/4 cups (300 mL). Serves 2.

1 serving: 96 Calories; 0.4 g Total Fat (0.1 g Mono, 0.1 g Poly, 0.1 g Sat); 0 mg Cholesterol; 22 g Carbohydrate; 6 g Fibre; 3 g Protein; 133 mg Sodium

Pictured on page 144.

 tip   Don't get caught red handed! Wear rubber gloves when handling beets.

Spiced Pecan Carrots

These tender carrots are made extra-special with the addition of a sweet and nutty topping. Pleasant cinnamon and nutmeg accents round out the flavour perfectly for a side that complements a wide range of dishes.

Thinly sliced carrot	1 cup	250 mL
(1/4 inch, 6 mm, thick)		
Water	1/2 cup	125 mL
Brown sugar, packed	1 tsp.	5 mL
Butter (or hard margarine)	1 tsp.	5 mL
Ground nutmeg, just a pinch		
Salt, just a pinch		
TOPPING		
Chopped pecans	1 1/2 tbsp.	25 mL
Brown sugar, packed	1 tsp.	5 mL
Butter (or hard margarine)	1/2 tsp.	2 mL
Ground cinnamon	1/4 tsp.	1 mL
Salt, just a pinch		

Combine first 6 ingredients in small saucepan. Cook, uncovered, on medium for about 15 minutes, stirring occasionally, until liquid is evaporated and carrot is tender-crisp. Toss carrot in pan for about 2 minutes until glazed. Transfer to serving dish.

Topping: Combine all 5 ingredients in small microwave-safe bowl. Microwave, uncovered, on high (100%) for about 1 minute until butter is melted and nuts are toasted. Stir. Scatter over carrot. Makes about 1 cup (250 mL). Serves 2.

1 serving: 107 Calories; 7.0 g Total Fat (3.0 g Mono, 1.4 g Poly, 2.2 g Sat); 8 mg Cholesterol; 12 g Carbohydrate; 2 g Fibre; 1 g Protein; 66 mg Sodium

Corn-Stuffed Tomatoes

Enjoy the summery flavours of sweet corn and tomatoes in a convenient and attractive side that you can make any day of the year.

Small tomatoes	2	2
Cooking oil	1 tsp.	5 mL
Finely chopped onion	1/4 cup	60 mL
Frozen kernel corn, thawed	3/4 cup	175 mL
Salt	1/8 tsp.	0.5 mL
Pepper, just a pinch		
Bacon slices, cooked crisp and crumbled	2	2
Chopped fresh chives (or green onion)	1 tbsp.	15 mL
Grated medium Cheddar cheese	3 tbsp.	50 mL
Chopped fresh chives (or green onion)	1 tsp.	5 mL

Trim 1/4 inch (6 mm) slice from tops of tomatoes. Using small spoon, scoop out seeds and pulp from tomatoes, leaving 1/4 inch (6 mm) thick shells. Discard seeds and pulp. Trim bottom of tomatoes to sit flat, being careful not to pierce shells. Place on greased baking sheet.

Heat cooking oil in small frying pan on medium-high. Add onion. Cook for about 3 minutes, stirring often, until onion is softened.

Add next 3 ingredients. Heat and stir for about 2 minutes until corn is heated through.

Add bacon and first amount of chives. Stir. Spoon into tomatoes.

Sprinkle with cheese. Bake in 450°F (230°C) oven for about 5 minutes until cheese is melted.

Sprinkle with second amount of chives. Makes 2 stuffed tomatoes.

1 stuffed tomato: 162 Calories; 8.9 g Total Fat (3.5 g Mono, 1.2 g Poly, 3.3 g Sat); 18 mg Cholesterol; 14 g Carbohydrate; 2 g Fibre; 7 g Protein; 365 mg Sodium

Potato Scallop

You don't need a crowd to enjoy creamy scalloped potatoes. Precooking the potatoes shortens the cooking time and ensures great results.

Butter (or hard margarine)	1 tbsp.	15 mL
Finely chopped onion	1/4 cup	60 mL
Salt	1/2 tsp.	2 mL
Milk	1 cup	250 mL
Bay leaf	1	1
Pepper, sprinkle		
Peeled baking potatoes, cut into 1/8 inch (3 mm) slices (see Note)	1 lb.	454 g
Grated Gruyère (or Cheddar) cheese	1/3 cup	75 mL

Melt butter in medium saucepan on medium. Add onion and salt. Cook for about 3 minutes, stirring often, until onion is softened.

Add next 3 ingredients. Stir. Add potato. Stir. Cook for about 2 minutes, stirring occasionally, until boiling. Reduce heat to medium-low. Simmer for 10 minutes, stirring occasionally. Discard bay leaf. Transfer to greased 2 cup (500 mL) baking dish. Smooth top. Bake, covered, in 375°F (190°C) oven for 15 minutes.

Sprinkle with cheese. Bake, uncovered, for about 20 minutes until potato is tender and cheese is golden. Makes about 2 cups (500 mL). Serves 2.

1 serving: 371 Calories; 13.0 g Total Fat (3.8 g Mono, 0.6 g Poly, 7.8 g Sat); 42 mg Cholesterol; 51 g Carbohydrate; 4 g Fibre; 14 g Protein; 762 mg Sodium

Note: Evenly sliced potatoes are one of the secrets to a good potato scallop. Use a mandolin slicer or food processor to ensure equal thickness.

Shiitake Risotto

A creamy risotto of earthy mushrooms and colourful veggies—the fantastic results certainly justify the effort! If you'd rather, other varieties of mushrooms could be used in place of shiitake.

Prepared vegetable broth	2 cups	500 mL
Cooking oil	1 tsp.	5 mL
Chopped fresh shiitake mushrooms	1/2 cup	125 mL
Finely chopped onion	1/3 cup	75 mL
Garlic clove, minced	1	1
(or 1/4 tsp., 1 mL, powder)		
Pepper	1/4 tsp.	1 mL
Arborio rice	1/3 cup	75 mL
Dry (or alcohol-free) white wine	1/4 cup	60 mL
Chopped sugar snap peas, trimmed	1/4 cup	60 mL
Finely chopped red pepper	1/4 cup	60 mL
Grated Parmesan cheese	2 tbsp.	30 mL
Chopped fresh parsley	1 tsp.	5 mL
(or 1/4 tsp., 1 mL, dried)		

Measure broth into small saucepan. Bring to a boil. Reduce heat to low. Cover to keep hot.

Heat cooking oil in medium saucepan on medium. Add next 4 ingredients. Cook for about 5 minutes, stirring often, until onion is softened.

Add rice. Stir until coated. Add wine. Heat and stir for about 1 minute until wine is absorbed. Add 1/2 cup (125 mL) hot broth, stirring constantly, until broth is absorbed. Repeat with remaining broth, 1/2 cup (125 mL) at a time, until all broth is absorbed and rice is tender. Add peas and red pepper with last addition of broth.

Add cheese. Stir well. Sprinkle with parsley. Makes about 1 1/2 cups (375 mL). Serves 2.

1 serving: 191 Calories; 4.8 g Total Fat (1.9 g Mono, 0.8 g Poly, 1.4 g Sat); 5 mg Cholesterol; 25 g Carbohydrate; 3 g Fibre; 6 g Protein; 586 mg Sodium

Pictured on page 108.

Stovetop Veggie Pilaf

Turn this mildly spiced combination of rice, colourful vegetables and bright flavours into a quick, light meal by adding some chopped cooked chicken.

Cooking oil	1 tsp.	5 mL
Finely chopped carrot	1/4 cup	60 mL
Finely chopped fresh green beans	1/4 cup	60 mL
Finely grated ginger root	1 tsp.	5 mL
(or 1/4 tsp., 1 mL, ground ginger)		
Turmeric	1/2 tsp.	2 mL
Prepared chicken broth	1 cup	250 mL
White basmati rice	1/2 cup	125 mL
Chopped fresh cilantro or parsley	1 tbsp.	15 mL
Finely chopped green onion	1 tbsp.	15 mL

Heat cooking oil in medium saucepan on medium. Add next 4 ingredients. Cook for about 4 minutes, stirring often, until vegetables are softened.

Add broth. Stir. Bring to a boil. Add rice. Stir. Reduce heat to medium-low. Simmer, covered, for 15 minutes, without stirring. Remove from heat. Let stand, covered, for about 5 minutes until rice is tender and liquid is absorbed. Fluff with fork.

Add cilantro and green onion. Stir. Makes about 2 cups (500 mL). Serves 2.

1 serving: 198 Calories; 3.5 g Total Fat (1.6 g Mono, 0.9 g Poly, 0.3 g Sat); 0 mg Cholesterol; 37 g Carbohydrate; 2 g Fibre; 4 g Protein; 754 mg Sodium

Creamy Green Beans

Instead of the old-fashioned and heavy green bean casserole, this lightened-up modern version can be quickly put together and has great visual appeal!

Salt, just a pinch		
Fresh (or frozen) cut green beans	1 1/2 cups	375 mL
Roasted red pepper, chopped	2 tbsp.	30 mL
Chive and onion cream cheese	1 tbsp.	15 mL
Dijon mustard (with whole seeds)	1 tsp.	5 mL

(continued on next page)

Sides

Pour water into medium frying pan until about 1 inch (2.5 cm) deep. Add salt. Bring to a boil. Add green beans. Reduce heat to medium. Boil gently, covered, for about 5 minutes until tender-crisp. Drain, reserving 1 tbsp. (15 mL) cooking liquid in small cup.

Add remaining 3 ingredients and reserved cooking liquid to beans. Heat and stir until coated. Makes about 1 2/3 cups (400 mL). Serves 2.

1 serving 70 Calories; 2.9 g Total Fat (0 g Mono, 0 g Poly, 1.8 g Sat); 8 mg Cholesterol; 8 g Carbohydrate; 3 g Fibre; 3 g Protein; 141 mg Sodium

Sweet Potato And Apple Mash

If you're already cooking something in the oven, you can cook the sweet potato at the same time. Just bake it for an hour or so until tender. This comforting side goes particularly well with roast pork.

Fresh unpeeled orange-fleshed sweet potato	1 lb.	454 g
Unsweetened applesauce	1/4 cup	60 mL
Butter (or hard margarine), softened	1 tbsp.	15 mL
Chopped fresh oregano (or 1/4 tsp., 1 mL, dried)	1 tsp.	5 mL
Salt	1/4 tsp.	1 mL
Pepper	1/4 tsp.	1 mL

Prick sweet potato in several places with a fork. Microwave, uncovered, on high (100%) for about 10 minutes, turning at halftime, until tender. Wrap in tea towel. Let stand for 5 minutes. Unwrap. Let stand for about 5 minutes until cool enough to handle. Cut sweet potato in half lengthwise. Scoop pulp into medium bowl. Discard shells. Mash pulp.

Add remaining 5 ingredients. Mash. Makes about 1 1/2 cups (375 mL). Serves 2.

1 serving: 303 Calories; 6.4 g Total Fat (1.5 g Mono, 0.5 g Poly, 3.8 g Sat); 15 mg Cholesterol; 59 g Carbohydrate; 7 g Fibre; 4 g Protein; 363 mg Sodium

Pictured on page 108.

Herbed Focaccia

*A warm piece of homemade focaccia and a salad make a
great casual weekend meal.*

Warm water	2/3 cup	150 mL
Granulated sugar	1/2 tsp.	2 mL
Dry active yeast	1 1/4 tsp.	6 mL
Olive oil	2 tbsp.	30 mL
All-purpose flour	1 1/2 cups	375 mL
Italian seasoning	1 tbsp.	15 mL
Salt	3/4 tsp.	4 mL
All-purpose flour, approximately	1/4 cup	60 mL
Olive oil	1/2 tsp.	2 mL

Stir warm water and sugar in small bowl until dissolved. Sprinkle yeast over top. Let stand for 10 minutes. Stir until yeast is dissolved.

Stir in first amount of olive oil.

Combine next 3 ingredients in large bowl. Make a well in centre. Add yeast mixture to well. Stir until soft dough forms. Turn out onto lightly floured surface. Knead for about 10 minutes until smooth and elastic, adding second amount of flour 1 tbsp. (15 mL) at a time, if necessary, to prevent sticking. Place in greased large bowl, turning once to grease top. Cover with greased waxed paper and tea towel. Let stand in oven with light on and door closed for about 45 minutes until doubled in bulk. Punch down dough. Turn out onto lightly floured surface. Knead for about 1 minute until smooth. Gently press dough into greased 9 inch (22 cm) round pan. Cover with greased waxed paper and tea towel. Let stand in oven with light on and door closed for about 30 minutes until doubled in size. Poke indentations on surface of dough with fingers.

Brush with second amount of olive oil. Bake in 400°F (205°C) oven for about 20 minutes until lightly browned. Remove from pan and place on wire rack to cool. Cuts into 6 wedges.

1 wedge: 165 Calories; 5.4 g Total Fat (3.9 g Mono, 0.8 g Poly, 0.8 g Sat); 0 mg Cholesterol; 26 g Carbohydrate; 1 g Fibre; 4 g Protein; 291 mg Sodium

Pictured on page 125.

Cranberry Apple Cake

Both tart and sweet, this moist cake is best served warm on a cold winter's night.

Brown sugar, packed	1/4 cup	60 mL
Butter (or hard margarine), softened	1 tbsp.	15 mL
Chopped frozen cranberries, thawed	1/4 cup	60 mL
Chopped peeled cooking apple (such as McIntosh)	1/4 cup	60 mL
All-purpose flour	1/2 cup	125 mL
Baking powder	1/2 tsp.	2 mL
Salt	1/8 tsp.	0.5 mL
Large egg, fork-beaten	1	1
Buttermilk (or soured milk, see Tip, page 137)	1/4 cup	60 mL
Brown sugar, packed	1/3 cup	75 mL
Cooking oil	1 1/2 tbsp.	25 mL
Vanilla extract	1/4 tsp.	1 mL

Combine first amount of brown sugar and butter in ungreased 7 x 3 inch (18 x 7.5 cm) foil loaf pan. Bake in 350°F (175°C) oven for about 5 minutes until sugar starts to bubble.

Scatter cranberry and apple over brown sugar mixture. Set aside.

Combine next 3 ingredients in medium bowl. Make a well in centre.

Combine remaining 5 ingredients in small bowl. Add to well. Stir until just moistened. Spread evenly over cranberry mixture. Bake for about 35 minutes until wooden pick inserted in centre of cake comes out clean. Let stand on wire rack for 5 minutes. Run knife around inside edge of pan. Invert onto serving plate. Cuts into 4 pieces.

1 piece: 278 Calories; 9.5 g Total Fat (3.8 g Mono, 1.6 g Poly, 2.7 g Sat); 63 mg Cholesterol; 46 g Carbohydrate; 1 g Fibre; 4 g Protein; 204 mg Sodium

Pictured on page 125.

Chocolate Oat Muffins

Chocolate, more chocolate and oats—this might just be the perfect breakfast!
Easy to wrap up and take with you for breakfast on the go.

All-purpose flour	3/4 cup	175 mL
Granulated sugar	1/2 cup	125 mL
Quick-cooking rolled oats	1/2 cup	125 mL
Cocoa powder, sifted if lumpy	2 tbsp.	30 mL
Baking powder	1 1/2 tsp.	7 mL
Salt	1/4 tsp.	1 mL
Large egg, fork-beaten	1	1
Buttermilk (or soured milk, see Tip, page 137)	1/2 cup	125 mL
Mini semi-sweet chocolate chips	1/4 cup	60 mL
Cooking oil	3 tbsp.	50 mL

Combine first 6 ingredients in medium bowl. Make a well in centre.

Combine remaining 4 ingredients in small bowl. Add to well. Stir until just moistened. Fill 6 greased muffin cups 3/4 full (see Tip, page 132). Bake in 375°F (190°C) oven for 18 to 20 minutes until wooden pick inserted in centre of muffin comes out clean. Let stand in pan for 5 minutes. Remove muffins from pan and place on wire rack to cool. Makes 6 muffins.

1 muffin: 263 Calories; 10.8 g Total Fat (4.8 g Mono, 2.1 g Poly, 2.3 g Sat); 37 mg Cholesterol; 39 g Carbohydrate; 1 g Fibre; 5 g Protein; 264 mg Sodium

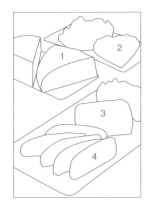

1. Herbed Focaccia, page 122
2. Veggie Pizza Bread, page 129
3. Cranberry Apple Cake, page 123
4. Chocolate Pistachio Biscotti, page 128

Spicy Southern Cornbread

This traditional cornbread contains no flour. The texture and taste are best straight from the oven, but if you happen to have some left over, warm it gently and serve with butter.

Grated jalapeño Monterey Jack cheese	1/2 cup	125 mL
Yellow cornmeal	1/2 cup	125 mL
Granulated sugar	1 tsp.	5 mL
Chili powder	1/2 tsp.	2 mL
Baking powder	1/4 tsp.	1 mL
Salt	1/4 tsp.	1 mL
Large egg, fork-beaten	1	1
Buttermilk (or soured milk, see Tip, page 137)	1/3 cup	75 mL

Combine first 6 ingredients in medium bowl. Make a well in centre.

Whisk egg and buttermilk in small bowl. Add to well. Stir until just moistened. Heat 2 cup (500 mL) baking dish in 450°F (230°C) oven for 3 minutes. Remove from oven. Spray with cooking spray. Pour batter into baking dish. Bake for about 15 minutes until firm and wooden pick inserted in centre comes out clean. Serve immediately. Cuts into 4 wedges.

1 wedge: 139 Calories; 6.4 g Total Fat (0.7 g Mono, 0.4 g Poly, 3.2 g Sat); 67 mg Cholesterol; 15 g Carbohydrate; 1 g Fibre; 7 g Protein; 521 mg Sodium

1. Layered Fiesta Dip, page 26
2. Prosciutto-Wrapped Chicken, page 24
3. Chèvre-Stuffed Mushrooms, page 28
4. Warm Shrimp Bruschetta, page 27

Props courtesy of: Winners Stores

Chocolate Pistachio Biscotti

And you thought it couldn't be done! We've created a small-yield recipe for biscotti. Now you can enjoy these crunchy cookies without making a huge amount or turning to store-bought varieties.

All-purpose flour	1 cup	250 mL
Coarsely chopped pistachios, toasted (see Tip, page 103)	1/4 cup	60 mL
Cocoa, sifted if lumpy	2 tbsp.	30 mL
Baking powder	1/4 tsp.	1 mL
Salt, just a pinch		
Butter (or hard margarine)	2 tbsp.	30 mL
Semi-sweet chocolate baking square (1 oz., 28 g), chopped	1	1
Granulated sugar	1/4 cup	60 mL
Large egg	1	1
Vanilla extract	1/4 tsp.	1 mL

Combine first 5 ingredients in medium bowl. Make a well in centre.

Put butter and chocolate into small microwave-safe bowl. Microwave on medium (50%), stirring every 15 seconds, until almost melted. Stir until smooth.

Beat sugar and chocolate mixture until combined. Beat in egg and vanilla. Add to well. Stir until soft dough forms. Turn out onto lightly floured surface. Knead for 1 to 2 minutes until smooth. Roll into 8 inch (20 cm) log. Place on greased cookie sheet. Flatten slightly to 3/4 inch (2 cm) thickness. Bake in 350°F (175°C) oven for about 35 minutes until edges are crisp. Let stand on cookie sheet for about 10 minutes until cool enough to handle. Using serrated knife, cut diagonally into 1/2 inch (12 mm) slices. Arrange, cut-side down, on greased cookie sheet. Reduce heat to 275°F (140°C). Bake for about 20 minutes until bottoms are crisp. Turn slices over. Turn oven off. Let stand in oven for about 30 minutes until dry and crisp. Makes about 10 biscotti.

1 biscotti: 126 Calories; 5.1 g Total Fat (1.4 g Mono, 0.5 g Poly, 2.3 g Sat); 28 mg Cholesterol; 18 g Carbohydrate; 1 g Fibre; 3 g Protein; 353 mg Sodium

Pictured on page 125.

Veggie Pizza Bread

A kaleidoscope of colourful veggies is packed into a pizza-flavoured bread.
Serve with a bowl of soup or salad for a complete meal.

All-purpose flour	1 cup	250 mL
Baking powder	1 1/2 tsp.	7 mL
Italian seasoning	1 tsp.	5 mL
Garlic salt	1/2 tsp.	2 mL
Baking soda	1/4 tsp.	1 mL
Large egg, fork-beaten	1	1
Milk	1/4 cup	60 mL
Granulated sugar	2 tsp.	10 mL
Grated medium Cheddar cheese	1/2 cup	125 mL
Chopped Roma (plum) tomato, seeds removed	1/4 cup	60 mL
Grated carrot	1/4 cup	60 mL
Grated zucchini (with peel)	1/4 cup	60 mL
Diced red pepper	2 tbsp.	15 mL
Sliced green onion	2 tbsp.	15 mL

Combine first 5 ingredients in medium bowl. Make a well in centre.

Combine next 3 ingredients in small bowl. Add to well.

Add remaining 6 ingredients to well. Stir until just moistened. Spoon into mound on greased baking sheet. Bake in 375°F (190°C) oven for about 25 minutes until golden and wooden pick inserted in centre of loaf comes out clean. Remove bread from baking sheet and place on wire rack. Let stand for 5 minutes. Serve warm. Cuts into 6 wedges.

1 wedge: 135 Calories; 4.0 g Total Fat (1.0 g Mono, 0.1 g Poly, 2.3 g Sat); 46 mg Cholesterol; 19 g Carbohydrate; 1 g Fibre; 6 g Protein; 506 mg Sodium

Pictured on page 125.

Golden Bread Crown

Speckled with flaxseed and beautifully twisted into a crown, this bread is sure to impress. The fancy presentation is not as fussy as you might think!

Milk	3/4 cup	175 mL
Granulated sugar	1/4 tsp.	1 mL
Active dry yeast	1 tsp.	5 mL
Olive oil	2 tsp.	10 mL
Whole-wheat flour	1 cup	250 mL
All-purpose flour	1/2 cup	125 mL
Ground flaxseed	1 tbsp.	15 mL
Salt	1/2 tsp.	2 mL
All-purpose flour, approximately	2 tbsp.	30 mL
Olive oil	1 tsp.	5 mL
Flaxseed	1/2 tsp.	2 mL
Coarse salt, sprinkle		

Combine milk and sugar in small heavy saucepan. Heat and stir on medium until very warm and sugar is dissolved. Pour into small bowl. Let stand for about 5 minutes until slightly cooled.

Sprinkle yeast over top. Let stand for 5 minutes.

Add first amount of olive oil. Stir until yeast is dissolved.

Combine next 4 ingredients in medium bowl. Make a well in centre. Add yeast mixture to well. Stir until soft dough forms. Turn out onto lightly floured surface. Knead for about 5 minutes until smooth and elastic, adding second amount of all-purpose flour 1 tbsp. (15 mL) at a time, if necessary, to prevent sticking. Place in greased large bowl, turning once to grease top. Cover with greased waxed paper and tea towel. Let stand in oven with light on and door closed for about 30 minutes until doubled in bulk. Punch dough down. Turn out onto lightly floured surface. Knead for about 1 minute until smooth. Divide into 2 equal portions. Roll each portion into 16 inch (40 cm) rope. Lay ropes, side-by-side, along length of greased baking sheet. Pinch ropes together at one end. Twist ropes around each other. Pinch together at opposite end. Shape into ring. Pinch ends together to seal. Cover with greased waxed paper and tea towel. Let stand in oven with light on and door closed for about 30 minutes until doubled in size.

(continued on next page)

Brush with second amount of olive oil. Sprinkle with flaxseed and coarse salt. Bake in 375°F (190°C) oven for about 20 minutes until golden brown and hollow-sounding when tapped. Let stand on baking sheet for 5 minutes before removing to wire rack to cool. Cuts into 4 wedges.

1 wedge: 226 Calories; 4.9 g Total Fat (2.8 g Mono, 0.7 g Poly, 0.9 g Sat); 3 mg Cholesterol; 39 g Carbohydrate; 5 g Fibre; 8 g Protein; 317 mg Sodium

Pictured on page 54.

Lemon Pecan Shortbread

Rich and buttery shortbread with a burst of fresh lemon and crunchy toasted nuts—a totally modern twist on this traditional cookie.

Butter, softened	1/4 cup	60 mL
Icing (confectioner's) sugar	2 tbsp.	30 mL
All-purpose flour	1/2 cup	125 mL
Finely chopped pecans, toasted	2 tbsp.	30 mL
(see Tip, page 103)		
Grated lemon zest	1/4 tsp.	1 mL
Salt, just a pinch		

Cream butter and icing sugar in small bowl.

Add remaining 4 ingredients. Stir until combined. Press into ungreased 6 inch (15 cm) pie plate. Prick cross pattern into dough with fork through to bottom of pan. Bake in 300°F (150°C) oven for about 30 minutes until just golden. Let stand in pan on wire rack for 5 minutes. Cuts into 4 wedges.

1 wedge: 191 Calories; 14.0 g Total Fat (4.5 g Mono, 1.2 g Poly, 7.4 g Sat); 30 mg Cholesterol; 15 g Carbohydrate; 1 g Fibre; 2 g Protein; 81 mg Sodium

Olive Cheddar Swirl Rolls

These cheesy little buns have flavours reminiscent of those fancy artisan breads from the bakery, combined with a unique presentation. Hot from your oven with minimal effort.

Frozen unbaked dinner rolls, covered, thawed in refrigerator overnight	2	2
Black olive tapenade	1 tbsp.	15 mL
Grated sharp Cheddar cheese	1/4 cup	60 mL
Grated sharp Cheddar cheese	2 tbsp.	30 mL

Roll out 1 dough portion on lightly floured surface to 4 inch (10 cm) square. Spread 1 1/2 tsp. (7 mL) tapenade over top. Sprinkle with 2 tbsp. (30 mL) of first amount of cheese. Roll up, jelly-roll style. Press seam against roll to seal. Cut into 4 slices. Arrange, cut-side up, in greased mini-muffin cups (see Tip, below). Repeat with remaining dough, tapenade and remaining first amount of cheese. Cover with greased waxed paper and tea towel. Let stand in oven with light on and door closed for about 1 hour until doubled in size.

Sprinkle with second amount of cheese. Bake in 375°F (190°C) oven for about 12 minutes until golden brown. Makes 8 rolls.

2 rolls: 98 Calories; 4.9 g Total Fat (1.0 g Mono, 0.1 g Poly, 2.3 g Sat); 11 mg Cholesterol; 9 g Carbohydrate; 1 g Fibre; 4 g Protein; 206 mg Sodium

Variation: Try using Asiago, havarti or Swiss cheese instead of sharp Cheddar.

 When making less than a full 12-cup pan of muffins, use the centre cups for even baking.

Sweet Potato Muffins

Lightly spiced and with beautiful yellow-orange tops, these gems are sure to satisfy your sweet tooth. Sweet potato adds great flavour and colour to these moist little muffins.

All-purpose flour	3/4 cup	175 mL
Baking powder	1/2 tsp.	2 mL
Ground cinnamon	1/2 tsp.	2 mL
Ground nutmeg	1/4 tsp.	1 mL
Salt	1/8 tsp.	0.5 mL
Large egg, fork-beaten	1	1
Mashed orange-fleshed sweet potato (see Note)	1/2 cup	125 mL
Granulated sugar	1/3 cup	75 mL
Butter (or hard margarine), melted	1/4 cup	60 mL
Milk	2 tbsp.	30 mL
Vanilla extract	1/2 tsp.	2 mL

Combine first 5 ingredients in medium bowl. Make a well in centre.

Combine remaining 6 ingredients in small bowl. Add to well. Stir until just moistened. Fill 6 greased muffin cups 3/4 full (see Tip, page 132). Bake in 375°F (190°C) oven for 18 to 20 minutes until wooden pick inserted in centre of muffin comes out clean. Let stand in pan for 5 minutes. Remove muffins from pan and place on wire rack to cool. Makes 6 muffins.

1 muffin: 192 Calories; 8.4 g Total Fat (2.0 g Mono, 0.3 g Poly, 5.1 g Sat); 56 mg Cholesterol; 26 g Carbohydrate; 1 g Fibre; 3 g Protein; 168 mg Sodium

Note: You can use canned sweet potato, mashed until smooth. If you have fresh orange-fleshed sweet potato on hand, just microwave until soft, then peel and mash.

Cinnamon Nut Swirl Bread

This sweet little loaf is packed with plenty of nuts and raisins and a hint of cinnamon. The perfect treat for a cool autumn day.

Frozen unbaked dinner rolls, covered, thawed in refrigerator overnight	2	2
Butter, softened	2 tsp.	10 mL
Chopped pecans	2 tbsp.	30 mL
Raisins	2 tbsp.	30 mL
Brown sugar, packed	1 tbsp.	15 mL
Ground cinnamon	1/4 tsp.	1 mL
Icing (confectioner's) sugar	3 tbsp.	50 mL
Orange juice (or milk)	1 tsp.	5 mL

Roll out dough on lightly floured surface, pressing portions together at one edge to make 6 x 9 inch (15 x 22 cm) rectangle.

Spread with butter. Combine next 4 ingredients in small bowl. Sprinkle over dough, almost to edges. Roll up, jelly-roll style, starting at 1 short edge. Place, seam-side down, in greased 6 x 3 1/2 x 2 inch (15 x 9 x 5 cm) foil loaf pan, tucking ends under. Cover with greased waxed paper and tea towel. Let stand in oven with light on and door closed for 1 hour. Using sharp knife, cut slits across top. Bake in 375°F (190°C) oven for about 18 minutes until golden brown and hollow sounding when tapped. Let stand in pan for 5 minutes. Remove bread from pan and place on wire rack to cool.

Stir icing sugar and orange juice in small bowl until smooth. Drizzle over loaf. Cuts into 6 slices.

1 slice: 95 Calories; 3.5 g Total Fat (1.3 g Mono, 0.6 g Poly, 1.0 g Sat); 3 mg Cholesterol; 15 g Carbohydrate; 1 g Fibre; 1 g Protein; 74 mg Sodium

Baking

Banana Streusel Cake

Banana bread is always a favourite, and this cake version is made even better with the addition of a sweet streusel topping. Makes a great breakfast or snack!

All-purpose flour	1/2 cup	125 mL
Baking powder	1/2 tsp.	2 mL
Baking soda	1/4 tsp.	1 mL
Salt	1/8 tsp.	0.5 mL
Butter (or hard margarine)	2 tbsp.	30 mL
Brown sugar, packed	1/4 cup	60 mL
Egg white (large)	1	1
Vanilla extract	1/4 tsp.	60 mL
Mashed overripe banana	1/3 cup	75 mL
(about 1/2 medium)		
Buttermilk (or powder, reconstituted)	2 tbsp.	30 mL
Finely chopped pecans	2 tbsp.	30 mL
Brown sugar, packed	2 tsp.	10 mL
Ground cinnamon, just a pinch		

Combine first 4 ingredients in medium bowl. Make a well in centre.

Cream butter and first amount of brown sugar in small bowl. Add egg white and vanilla. Beat well.

Add banana and buttermilk. Stir. Add to well. Stir until just moistened. Spread in greased 5 1/8 x 4 1/16 x 1 5/8 inch (13 x 10 x 4 cm) foil pan.

Combine remaining 3 ingredients in small cup. Sprinkle over banana mixture. Bake in 375°F (190°C) oven for about 30 minutes until wooden pick inserted in centre of cake comes out clean. Let stand in pan on wire rack for 5 minutes. Cuts into 4 pieces.

1 piece: 214 Calories; 8.6 g Total Fat (3.0 g Mono, 1.0 g Poly, 3.9 g Sat); 16 mg Cholesterol; 32 g Carbohydrate; 1 g Fibre; 3 g Protein; 287 mg Sodium

Quick Molasses Loaf

Cozy up with a book, a cup of tea and a delectable piece of this sweet bread.

Whole-wheat flour	1 cup	250 mL
All-purpose flour	1/2 cup	125 mL
Baking powder	1 tsp.	5 mL
Baking soda	1/2 tsp.	2 mL
Salt	1/4 tsp.	1 mL
Large egg, fork-beaten	1	1
Buttermilk (or soured milk, see Tip, page 137)	3/4 cup	175 mL
Fancy (mild) molasses	1/3 cup	75 mL
Cooking oil	2 tbsp.	30 mL

Combine first 5 ingredients in medium bowl. Make a well in centre.

Combine remaining 4 ingredients in small bowl. Add to well. Stir until just moistened. Spread in greased 7 x 3 inch (18 x 7.5 cm) foil loaf pan. Bake in 375°F (190°C) oven for about 35 minutes until wooden pick inserted in centre comes out clean. Let stand in pan for 5 minutes. Remove loaf from pan and place on wire rack to cool. Cuts into 8 slices.

1 slice: 168 Calories; 4.8 g Total Fat (2.2 g Mono, 1.1 g Poly, 0.8 g Sat); 29 mg Cholesterol; 28 g Carbohydrate; 2 g Fibre; 5 g Protein; 254 mg Sodium

Cranberry Butter Tarts

These sweet and easy tarts are always a favourite, and are particularly good for serving with tea. They also make the perfect end to a holiday meal.

Unbaked tart shells	4	4
Dried cranberries	1/4 cup	60 mL
Chopped sliced almonds	2 tbsp.	30 mL
Egg yolk (large), fork-beaten	1	1
Brown sugar, packed	3 tbsp.	50 mL
Butter, melted	1 tbsp.	15 mL
Almond extract	1/4 tsp.	1 mL

(continued on next page)

Arrange tart shells on foil-lined baking sheet. Sprinkle cranberries and almonds into shells.

Combine remaining 4 ingredients in small bowl. Spoon over cranberries. Bake in 375°F (190°C) oven until pastry is golden and filling is almost set. Let stand on wire rack for 15 minutes. Makes 4 tarts.

1 tart: 199 Calories; 10.2 g Total Fat (2.3 g Mono, 0.7 g Poly, 4.3 g Sat); 62 mg Cholesterol; 26 g Carbohydrate; 1 g Fibre; 2 g Protein; 91 mg Sodium

Herbed Scones

Rather than serving ordinary store-bought buns, these simple scones make a much tastier dinner companion for stew, soup or pasta.

Whole-wheat flour	1 cup	250 mL
Italian seasoning	1 tbsp.	15 mL
Baking powder	1 tsp.	5 mL
Salt	1/4 tsp.	1 mL
Half-and-half cream	1/2 cup	125 mL
Cooking oil	2 tbsp.	30 mL
Grated lemon zest	1/2 tsp.	2 mL

Measure first 4 ingredients into medium bowl. Stir. Make a well in centre.

Combine remaining 3 ingredients in small bowl. Add to well. Stir until just moistened. Drop, using about 1/4 cup (60 mL) for each scone, about 1 inch (2.5 cm) apart onto greased baking sheet. Bake in 400°F (205°C) oven for about 15 minutes until wooden pick inserted in centre of scone comes out clean. Makes 4 scones.

1 scone: 204 Calories; 11.0 g Total Fat (5.1 g Mono, 2.4 g Poly, 2.7 g Sat); 11 mg Cholesterol; 24 g Carbohydrate; 4 g Fibre; 5 g Protein; 297 mg Sodium

Pictured on page 89.

 tip To make soured milk, measure 1 1/2 tsp. (7 mL) white vinegar or lemon juice into a 1 cup (250 mL) liquid measure. Add enough milk to make 1/2 cup (125 mL). Stir. Let stand for 5 minutes.

Baby Black Forest Cake

Don't have an electric mixer? Don't worry. You don't need one to make this rich and chocolatey cake. For added convenience, you could use ready-made whipped cream in place of the Chantilly Cream.

Cocoa, sifted if lumpy	1/2 tsp.	2 mL
Large egg, fork-beaten	1	1
Sour cream	2 tbsp.	30 mL
All-purpose flour	1/4 cup	60 mL
Granulated sugar	3 tbsp.	50 mL
Baking soda	1/8 tsp.	0.5 mL
Salt, just a pinch		
Butter (or hard margarine)	2 tbsp.	30 mL
Cocoa, sifted if lumpy	2 tbsp.	30 mL
Hot strong prepared coffee	2 tbsp.	30 mL
CHANTILLY CREAM		
Whipping cream	1/2 cup	125 mL
Icing (confectioner's) sugar	2 tbsp.	30 mL
Vanilla extract	1/8 tsp.	0.5 mL
Pitted sour cherries, halved	4	4
Cherry jam	2 tbsp.	30 mL
Cherry liqueur	1 tsp.	5 mL
Pitted sour cherries, halved	8	8

Grease 4 1/2 inch (11 cm) diameter round foil pan. Sprinkle with first amount of cocoa. Turn pan to coat bottom and sides. Discard excess cocoa.

Combine egg and sour cream in small bowl. Set aside.

Combine next 4 ingredients in medium bowl.

Combine next 3 ingredients in small saucepan on medium. Heat and stir until mixture is smooth and bubbling. Remove from heat. Add sour cream mixture. Stir. Add to flour mixture. Whisk until smooth. Pour into prepared pan. Bake in 375°F (190°C) oven for about 25 minutes until wooden pick inserted in centre of cake comes out clean. Let stand for 10 minutes. Remove cake from pan and place on wire rack to cool completely.

Chantilly Cream: Beat first 3 ingredients in medium bowl until stiff peaks form.

(continued on next page)

Desserts

Fold in first amount of cherries until just combined. Makes about 3/4 cup (175 mL) cream.

Combine jam and liqueur in small cup.

Cut cake horizontally into 2 equal layers (see Note). To assemble, layer ingredients on serving plate as follows:

1. 1 cake layer, cut-side up
2. Half of jam mixture
3. Half of Chantilly Cream
4. Remaining cake layer, cut-side down
5. Remaining jam mixture
6. Remaining Chantilly Cream

Top with second amount of cherries. Cuts into 4 wedges.

1 wedge: 234 Calories; 10.4 g Total Fat (1.5 g Mono, 0.2 g Poly, 6.4 g Sat); 84 mg Cholesterol; 31 g Carbohydrate; 1 g Fibre; 3 g Protein; 99 mg Sodium

Pictured on page 143.

Note: To cut cake layers evenly, place a piece of fine string or strong thread about 5 inches (12.5 cm) longer than the circumference of the cake around the outside edge. Bring both ends of the string around to the front of the cake. Cross the ends of the string in front and, checking that the string is level, firmly pull the ends in opposite directions to cut through the cake.

Buttered Pecan Whip

This rich and creamy whipped dessert comes in small portions, and that's all you'll need. Serve in stemware for an elegant presentation.

Butter	1/2 tsp.	2 mL
Pecan pieces	2 tbsp.	30 mL
Mascarpone cheese	1/3 cup	75 mL
Brown sugar, packed	1/4 cup	60 mL
Whipping cream	1/3 cup	75 mL

Melt butter in small frying pan on medium. Add pecans. Heat and stir for about 3 minutes until golden. Cool.

Beat cheese and brown sugar in small bowl on low until combined. Beat on high for 1 minute. Add whipping cream. Beat on high for about 1 minute until light and fluffy. Spoon into bowls. Sprinkle with pecans. Chill for about 20 minutes until set. Makes about 1 1/4 cups (300 mL). Serves 2.

1 serving: 386 Calories; 28.7 g Total Fat (3.3 g Mono, 1.6 g Poly, 13.7 g Sat); 69 mg Cholesterol; 31 g Carbohydrate; 0.7 g Fibre; 4 g Protein; 40 mg Sodium

Desserts

Warm Gingered Pear Cake

Although this dessert may seem a little old-fashioned, the combination of ginger and pear in a warm cake makes for the ultimate comfort food. A bit of maple sweetness rounds out the flavour.

Diced peeled pear	1 cup	250 mL
Minced crystallized ginger	1/2 tsp.	2 mL
Maple (or maple-flavoured) syrup	1 tsp.	5 mL
All-purpose flour	3 tbsp.	50 mL
Brown sugar, packed	1 tbsp.	15 mL
Baking powder	1/4 tsp.	1 mL
Ground ginger	1/8 tsp.	0.5 mL
Salt, sprinkle		
Large egg	1	1
Milk	1 1/2 tsp.	7 mL
Cooking oil	1/2 tsp.	2 mL
Minced crystallized ginger	1/2 tsp.	2 mL
Maple (or maple-flavoured) syrup	2 tsp.	10 mL

Divide pear and first amounts of crystallized ginger and maple syrup into 2 greased 6 oz. (170 mL) ramekins. Bake in 350°F (175°C) oven for 10 minutes.

Combine next 5 ingredients in small bowl. Stir.

Whisk next 4 ingredients in separate small bowl until frothy. Add to flour mixture. Whisk until smooth. Pour into ramekins. Bake for about 20 minutes until golden and wooden pick inserted in centre of cake comes out clean. Let stand for 5 minutes.

Drizzle with second amount of maple syrup. Serve warm. Serves 2.

1 serving: 187 Calories; 3.6 g Total Fat (0.7 g Mono, 0.4 g Poly, 0.9 g Sat); 108 mg Cholesterol; 36 g Carbohydrate; 3 g Fibre; 5 g Protein; 108 mg Sodium

Croissant Bread Pudding

This miniature bread pudding is the perfect solution when you've got a couple of lonely, day-old croissants lingering in the bread bin.

Large egg, fork-beaten	1	1
Egg yolk (large)	1	1
Evaporated milk (or half-and-half cream)	1/4 cup	60 mL
Coffee-flavoured liqueur	1 tbsp.	15 mL
Granulated sugar	1 tbsp.	15 mL
Vanilla extract	1/4 tsp.	1 mL
Salt, just a pinch		
Medium croissants, torn into 1 inch (2.5 cm) pieces	2	2
Evaporated milk (or half-and-half cream)	1/4 cup	60 mL
Coffee-flavoured liqueur	1 tbsp.	15 mL
Cocoa, sifted if lumpy, for garnish		

Combine first 7 ingredients in medium bowl. Add croissant pieces. Stir. Let stand for 10 minutes. Transfer to greased 2 cup (500 mL) casserole. Bake, covered, in 325°F (160°C) oven for 30 minutes. Bake, uncovered, for about 10 minutes until top is golden and knife inserted in centre comes out clean.

Combine second amount of evaporated milk and liqueur in small bowl. Drizzle over pudding.

Dust with cocoa. Serves 2.

1 serving: 414 Calories; 18.5 g Total Fat (1.8 g Mono, 0.5 g Poly, 10.6 g Sat); 260 mg Cholesterol; 42 g Carbohydrate; 1 g Fibre; 11 g Protein; 288 mg Sodium

Paré Pointer

My dog is pretty dirty, but he's even prettier when he's clean.

Raspberry Meringue Nests

A crisp, sweet meringue provides the perfect nest to hold a filling of tart raspberries and sweet cream.

Egg white (large), room temperature	1	1
Cream of tartar	1/8 tsp.	0.5 mL
Salt, just a pinch		
Granulated sugar	1/4 cup	60 mL
Vanilla extract	1/4 tsp.	1 mL
Fresh (or frozen, thawed) raspberries	1/2 cup	125 mL
Granulated sugar	1/4 tsp.	1 mL
Frozen whipped topping, thawed	1/2 cup	125 mL

Line bottom of baking sheet with parchment (not waxed) paper. Trace two 4 inch (10 cm) diameter circles about 1 1/2 inches (3.8 cm) apart on paper. Turn paper over. Beat first 3 ingredients in small bowl until soft peaks form.

Add first amount of sugar, 1 tbsp. (15 mL) at a time, beating well after each addition, until stiff peaks form. Add vanilla with last addition of sugar. Spoon egg white mixture onto circles. Spread evenly. Create nests by pushing some of meringue mixture from centre out to sides to create edges. Bake in 225°F (110°C) oven for about 1 hour until dry. Turn oven off. Let stand in oven with door slightly ajar until completely cooled.

Spoon raspberries into nests. Sprinkle with second amount of sugar. Spoon whipped topping over raspberries. Serves 2.

1 serving: 172 Calories; 4.0 g Total Fat (0 g Mono, 0 g Poly, 4.0 g Sat); 0 mg Cholesterol; 34 g Carbohydrate; 0 g Fibre; 2 g Protein; 38 mg Sodium

1. Creamy Raspberry Dessert, page 148
2. Chocolate Caramel Cupcakes, page 146
3. Baby Black Forest Cake, page 138

Desserts

Chocolate Cheesecake Cups

This dessert's just right for those times when you want a sweet bite at the end of a meal, without a whole cheesecake hanging around to tempt you later.

CRUST
Butter (or hard margarine)	2 tsp.	10 mL
Graham cracker crumbs	2 tbsp.	30 mL
Brown sugar, packed	1 tsp.	5 mL
Cocoa, sifted if lumpy	1 tsp.	5 mL

FILLING
Cream cheese, softened	4 oz.	125 g
Granulated sugar	1 1/2 tbsp.	25 mL
Cocoa, sifted if lumpy	1 tbsp.	15 mL
Milk	1 tbsp.	15 mL
Vanilla extract	1/4 tsp.	1 mL

Crust: Put butter into small microwave-safe cup. Microwave on high (100%) for 10 to 15 seconds until melted. Add remaining 3 ingredients. Stir well. Press into 2 greased 6 oz. (170 mL) custard cups.

Filling: Beat all 5 ingredients in small bowl until smooth. Spread evenly over graham crumb mixture. Chill, covered, for at least 8 hours or overnight. Serves 2.

1 serving: 319 Calories; 24.7 g Total Fat (1.2 g Mono, 0.3 g Poly, 14.5 g Sat); 71 mg Cholesterol; 20 g Carbohydrate; 1 g Fibre; 5 g Protein; 244 mg Sodium

1. Roast Cornish Hen, page 62
2. Orange Mint Beets, page 115

Props courtesy of: The Bay

Chocolate Caramel Cupcakes

These moist cupcakes will finally put the debate to rest—which is better, caramel or chocolate? The answer is simple. Combine the two for the best of both worlds!

All-purpose flour	1/2 cup	125 mL
Granulated sugar	1/3 cup	75 mL
Cocoa, sifted if lumpy	2 tbsp.	30 mL
Baking soda	1/4 tsp.	1 mL
Salt	1/4 tsp.	1 mL
Large egg, fork-beaten	1	1
Buttermilk (or soured milk, see Tip, page 137)	1/3 cup	75 mL
Butter (or hard margarine), melted	2 tbsp.	30 mL
Vanilla extract	1/4 tsp.	1 mL
CARAMEL ICING		
Brown sugar, packed	1/2 cup	125 mL
Butter (or hard margarine)	1/4 cup	60 mL
Milk	2 tbsp.	30 mL
Icing (confectioner's) sugar	1 cup	250 mL
Vanilla extract	1/2 tsp.	2 mL

Combine first 5 ingredients in medium bowl. Stir. Make a well in centre.

Combine remaining 4 ingredients in small bowl. Add to well. Stir until just moistened. Fill 4 greased muffin cups 3/4 full (see Tip, page 132). Bake in 375°F (190°C) oven for about 15 minutes until wooden pick inserted in centre of cupcake comes out clean. Let stand in pan for 5 minutes. Remove cupcakes from pan and place on to wire rack to cool.

Caramel Icing: Combine first 3 ingredients in medium saucepan. Bring to a boil on medium. Reduce heat to medium-low. Simmer for 3 minutes. Remove from heat. Let stand for about 30 minutes until cool.

Add icing sugar and vanilla. Beat for about 2 minutes until spreading consistency. Makes about 3/4 cup (175 mL) icing. Spread over cupcakes. Makes 4 cupcakes.

1 cupcake: 531 Calories; 18.9 g Total Fat (4.6 g Mono, 0.7 g Poly, 11.5 g Sat); 101 mg Cholesterol; 88 g Carbohydrate; 1 g Fibre; 5 g Protein; 394 mg Sodium

Pictured on page 143.

Orange-Iced Brownies

Moist, decadent brownies with an orangey cream cheese icing. Just enough for two—but if you're feeling sinful, you could keep them all for yourself.

All-purpose flour	1/4 cup	60 mL
Granulated sugar	1/4 cup	60 mL
Cocoa, sifted if lumpy	2 tbsp.	30 mL
Salt	1/8 tsp.	0.5 mL
Large egg	1	1
Cooking oil	2 tbsp.	30 mL
ORANGE ICING		
Cream cheese, softened	1/4 cup	60 mL
Icing (confectioner's) sugar	1/4 cup	60 mL
Orange liqueur	1 tsp.	5 mL

Combine first 4 ingredients in medium bowl. Make a well in centre.

Whisk egg and cooking oil until combined. Add to well. Stir until just moistened. Pour into greased 5 inch (12.5 cm) foil pot pie plate. Bake in 350°F (175°C) oven for about 20 minutes until wooden pick inserted in centre comes out moist but not wet with batter. Do not overbake. Let stand in pan for 5 minutes. Remove brownie from pan and place on wire rack to cool.

Orange Icing: Beat all 3 ingredients in small bowl until spreading consistency. Makes about 1/3 cup (75 mL) icing. Spread over top and sides of cooled brownie. Cuts into 4 wedges.

1 wedge: 282 Calories; 17.1 g Total Fat (6.5 g Mono, 2.3 g Poly, 6.4 g Sat); 81 mg Cholesterol; 28 g Carbohydrate; 1 g Fibre; 5 g Protein; 163 mg Sodium

Paré Pointer

Our dog is like a baseball player. He runs for home when he sees the dog catcher coming.

Creamy Raspberry Dessert

It's hard to believe that something so delicious could come from a few simple ingredients! Be creative and try using any combination of jelly powder and liqueur that strikes your fancy.

Boiling water	1/2 cup	125 mL
Raspberry jelly powder (gelatin)	3 tbsp.	50 mL
Half-and-half cream	1/2 cup	125 mL
Raspberry (or orange) liqueur (optional)	2 tbsp.	30 mL
Fresh berries, for garnish		
Sprigs of fresh mint, for garnish		

Stir boiling water into jelly powder in small bowl until dissolved.

Add cream and liqueur. Stir. Pour into two 6 oz. (170 mL) dessert cups. Chill for about 2 hours until set.

Garnish with berries and mint sprigs. Serves 2.

1 serving: 136 Calories; 6.9 g Total Fat (2.0 g Mono, 0.3 g Poly, 4.3 g Sat); 22 mg Cholesterol; 16 g Carbohydrate; 0 g Fibre; 3 g Protein; 83 mg Sodium

Pictured on page 143.

Cinnamon Orange Crème Brûlée

Celebrate a special occasion with the ultimate in sinful desserts! Rich crème brûlée is made even better with the addition of chocolate and liqueur. Serve with a cup of coffee with a dash of orange liqueur.

Whipping cream	2/3 cup	150 mL
Cinnamon stick (4 inch, 10 cm, length)	1	1
Grated orange zest	1/2 tsp.	2 mL
White chocolate baking squares (1 oz., 28 g, each), chopped	2	2
Granulated sugar	1 tbsp.	15 mL
Egg yolks (large), fork-beaten	2	2
Orange liqueur	1 tsp.	5 mL
Granulated sugar	2 tsp.	10 mL

(continued on next page)

148 Desserts

Combine first 3 ingredients in small heavy saucepan on medium. Heat and stir for about 3 minutes until bubbles form around edge of saucepan. Remove from heat. Let stand, covered, for 5 minutes. Remove and discard cinnamon stick.

Add chocolate and first amount of sugar. Stir until chocolate is melted.

Add egg yolks and liqueur. Whisk until well combined. Place two 1/2 cup (125 mL) ovenproof ramekins in 8 x 8 inch (20 x 20 cm) baking dish. Pour egg mixture into ramekins. Carefully pour boiling water into pan until halfway up sides of ramekins. Bake in 300°F (150°C) oven for about 35 minutes until custards are set along edges but centres still wobble. Carefully remove ramekins from water. Place on wire rack to cool. Chill, covered, for at least 4 hours or overnight.

Sprinkle second amount of sugar evenly over tops. Broil on top rack in oven for about 4 minutes until sugar is bubbling and browned. Let stand for 5 minutes. Serves 2.

1 serving: 539 Calories; 42.9 g Total Fat (10.4 g Mono, 1.8 g Poly, 25.9 g Sat); 324 mg Cholesterol; 31 g Carbohydrate; trace Fibre; 6 g Protein; 69 mg Sodium

Cranberry Orange Delight

Delight your taste buds with a burst of flavour in this refreshing frozen dessert. A tart combination of cranberry and orange in the form of a simplified no-bake cheesecake!

CRUST
Butter (or hard margarine), melted	1 1/2 tbsp.	25 mL
Graham cracker crumbs	1/3 cup	75 mL
Granulated sugar	1 tbsp.	15 mL

FILLING
Jellied cranberry sauce	3/4 cup	175 mL
Cream cheese, softened	2 oz.	57 g
Orange liqueur	1 1/2 tsp.	7 mL
Grated orange zest	1/2 tsp.	2 mL

Crust: Combine all 3 ingredients in small bowl. Press evenly in bottom of greased 2 cup (500 mL) casserole. Chill for 30 minutes.

Filling: Beat all 4 ingredients in small bowl until smooth. Pour over crust. Freeze, uncovered, for about 1 hour until firm. Cuts into 4 wedges.

1 wedge: 215 Calories; 10.4 g Total Fat (2.9 g Mono, 0.6 g Poly, 6.2 g Sat); 28 mg Cholesterol; 29 g Carbohydrate; 1 g Fibre; 2 g Protein; 129 mg Sodium

Measurement Tables

Throughout this book measurements are given in Conventional and Metric measure. To compensate for differences between the two measurements due to rounding, a full metric measure is not always used. The cup used is the standard 8 fluid ounce. Temperature is given in degrees Fahrenheit and Celsius. Baking pan measurements are in inches and centimetres as well as quarts and litres. An exact metric conversion is given below as well as the working equivalent (Metric Standard Measure).

Spoons

Conventional Measure	Metric Exact Conversion Millilitre (mL)	Metric Standard Measure Millilitre (mL)
1/8 teaspoon (tsp.)	0.6 mL	0.5 mL
1/4 teaspoon (tsp.)	1.2 mL	1 mL
1/2 teaspoon (tsp.)	2.4 mL	2 mL
1 teaspoon (tsp.)	4.7 mL	5 mL
2 teaspoons (tsp.)	9.4 mL	10 mL
1 tablespoon (tbsp.)	14.2 mL	15 mL

Cups

Conventional Measure	Metric Exact Conversion Millilitre (mL)	Metric Standard Measure Millilitre (mL)
1/4 cup (4 tbsp.)	56.8 mL	60 mL
1/3 cup (5 1/3 tbsp.)	75.6 mL	75 mL
1/2 cup (8 tbsp.)	113.7 mL	125 mL
2/3 cup (10 2/3 tbsp.)	151.2 mL	150 mL
3/4 cup (12 tbsp.)	170.5 mL	175 mL
1 cup (16 tbsp.)	227.3 mL	250 mL
4 1/2 cups	1022.9 mL	1000 mL (1

Dry Measurements

Conventional Measure Ounces (oz.)	Metric Exact Conversion Grams (g)	Metric Standard Measure Grams (g)
1 oz.	28.3 g	28 g
2 oz.	56.7 g	57 g
3 oz.	85.0 g	85 g
4 oz.	113.4 g	125 g
5 oz.	141.7 g	140 g
6 oz.	170.1 g	170 g
7 oz.	198.4 g	200 g
8 oz.	226.8 g	250 g
16 oz.	453.6 g	500 g
32 oz.	907.2 g	1000 g (1 k(

Oven Temperatures

Fahrenheit (°F)	Celsius (°C)
175°	80°
200°	95°
225°	110°
250°	120°
275°	140°
300°	150°
325°	160°
350°	175°
375°	190°
400°	205°
425°	220°
450°	230°
475°	240°
500°	260°

Pans

Conventional Inches	Metric Centimetres
8x8 inch	20x20 cm
9x9 inch	22x22 cm
9x13 inch	22x33 cm
10x15 inch	25x38 cm
11x17 inch	28x43 cm
8x2 inch round	20x5 cm
9x2 inch round	22x5 cm
10x4 1/2 inch tube	25x11 cm
8x4x3 inch loaf	20x10x7.5 cm
9x5x3 inch loaf	22x12.5x7.5 cm

Casseroles

CANADA & BRITAIN		UNITED STATES	
Standard Size Casserole	Exact Metric Measure	Standard Size Casserole	Exact Metric Measure
1 qt. (5 cups)	1.13 L	1 qt. (4 cups)	900 ml
1 1/2 qts. (7 1/2 cups)	1.69 L	1 1/2 qts. (6 cups)	1.35 L
2 qts. (10 cups)	2.25 L	2 qts. (8 cups)	1.8 L
2 1/2 qts. (12 1/2 cups)	2.81 L	2 1/2 qts. (10 cups)	2.25 L
3 qts. (15 cups)	3.38 L	3 qts. (12 cups)	2.7 L
4 qts. (20 cups)	4.5 L	4 qts. (16 cups)	3.6 L
5 qts. (25 cups)	5.63 L	5 qts. (20 cups)	4.5 L

Recipe Index

155

156

Company's Coming cookbooks are available at retail locations throughout Canada!

EXCLUSIVE mail order offer on next page
Buy any 2 cookbooks—choose a 3rd FREE of equal or lesser value than the lowest price paid.

Original Series $15.99

CODE		CODE		CODE	
SQ	150 Delicious Squares	SCH	Stews, Chilies & Chowders	KHC	Kids' Healthy Cooking
CA	Casseroles	FD	Fondues	MM	Mostly Muffins
MU	Muffins & More	CCBE	The Beef Book	SP	Soups
SA	Salads	RC	The Rookie Cook	SU	Simple Suppers
AP	Appetizers	RHR	Rush-Hour Recipes	CCDC	Diabetic Cooking
CO	Cookies	SW	Sweet Cravings	CHN	Chicken Now
PA	Pasta	YRG	Year-Round Grilling	KDS	Kids Do Snacks
BA	Barbecues	GG	Garden Greens	TMRC	30-Minute Rookie Cook
PR	Preserves	CHC	Chinese Cooking	LFE	Low-Fat Express
CH	Chicken, Etc.	BEV	The Beverage Book	SI	Choosing Sides
CT	Cooking For Two	SCD	Slow Cooker Dinners	PAS	Perfect Pasta And Sauces
SC	Slow Cooker Recipes	WM	30-Minute Weekday Meals	TMDC	30-Minute Diabetic Cooking
SF	Stir-Fry	SDL	School Days Lunches	CCHH	Healthy in a Hurry
MAM	Make-Ahead Meals	PD	Potluck Dishes	TT	Table for Two **NEW** *Feb. 1/09*
PB	The Potato Book	GBR	Ground Beef Recipes		
CCLFC	Low-Fat Cooking	FRIR	4-Ingredient Recipes		

Cookbook Author Biography

CODE	$15.99
JP	Jean Paré: An Appetite for Life

Most Loved Recipe Collection

CODE	$23.99
MLBQ	Most Loved Barbecuing

CODE	$24.99
MLSD	Most Loved Salads & Dressings
MLCA	Most Loved Casseroles
MLSF	Most Loved Stir-Fries
MLHF	Most Loved Holiday Favourites
MLSC	Most Loved Slow Cooker Creations
MLDE	Most Loved Summertime Desserts
MLFB	Most Loved Festive Baking **NEW** *Nov. 1/08*

3-in-1 Cookbook Collection

CODE	$29.99
MME	Meals Made Easy

2-in-1 Cookbook Collection

CODE	$24.99
HECH	Healthy Choices
RCCP	The Rookie Cook's Companion **NEW** *Jan. 1/09*

Lifestyle Series

CODE	$19.99
DDI	Diabetic Dinners
HH	Healthy in a Hurry
WGR	Whole Grain Recipes

Special Occasion Series

CODE	$24.99
CGFK	Christmas Gifts from the Kitchen
TR	Timeless Recipes for All Occasions
CCT	Company's Coming–Tonight! **NEW** *Oct. 1/08*

CODE	$27.99
CCEL	Christmas Celebrations

CODE	$29.99
CATH	Cooking At Home

Practical Gourmet – NEW!

CODE	$29.99
SPFS	Small Plates for Sharing **NEW** *Sept. 1/08*

Order **ONLINE** for fast delivery!

Log onto **www.companyscoming.com**, browse through our library of cookbooks, gift sets and newest releases and place your order using our fast and secure online order form.

Buy 2, Get 1 FREE!

Buy any 2 cookbooks—choose a **3rd FREE** of equal or lesser value than the lowest price paid.

TITLE	CODE	QUANTITY	PRICE	TOTAL
			$	$

DON'T FORGET to indicate your FREE BOOK(S). (see exclusive mail order offer above) PLEASE PRINT

TOTAL BOOKS (including FREE)

TOTAL BOOKS PURCHASED

	INTERNATIONAL Canada Air Mail	USA	Canada
Shipping & Handling First Book (per destination)	$ .98 (one book)	$9.98 (one book)	$5.98 (one book)
Additional Books (include FREE books)	($7.99 each) $	($1.99 each) $	($1.99 each) $
Sub-Total	$	$	$
Canadian residents add GST/HST		$	$
TOTAL AMOUNT ENCLOSED	$	$	$

Terms
- All orders must be prepaid. Sorry, no CODs.
- Canadian orders are processed in Canadian funds, US International orders. are processed in US funds.
- Prices are subject to change without prior notice.
- Canadian residents must pay GST/HST (no provincial tax required).
- No tax is required for orders outside Canada.
- Satisfaction is guaranteed or return within 30 days for a full refund.
- Make cheque or money order payable to: **Company's Coming Publishing Limited** 2311-96 Street, Edmonton, Alberta Canada T6N 1G3.
- Orders are shipped surface mail. For courier rates, visit our website: **www.companyscoming.com** or contact us: **Tel: 780-450-6223 Fax: 780-450-1857.**

Gift Giving
- Let us help you with your gift giving!
- We will send cookbooks directly to the recipients of your choice if you give us their names and addresses.
- Please specify the titles you wish to send to each person.
- If you would like to include a personal note or card, we will be pleased to enclose it with your gift order.
- Company's Coming Cookbooks make excellent gifts: birthdays, bridal showers, Mother's Day, Father's Day, graduation or any occasion …collect them all!

☐ MasterCard ☐ VISA   Expiry ___/___ MO/YR

Credit Card # _____

Name of cardholder _____

Cardholder signature _____

Shipping Address Send the cookbooks listed above to:
☐ Please check if this is a Gift Order

Name: _____

Street: _____

City: _____ Prov./State: _____

Postal Code/Zip: _____ Country: _____

Tel: (   ) _____

E-mail address: _____

Your privacy is important to us. We will not share your e-mail address or personal information with any outside party

☐ **YES! Please add me to your News Bite e-mail newsletter.**

158

Cookmark

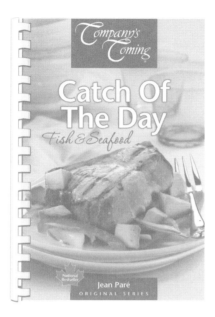

These all-new recipes reflect the popularity and ease of cooking with fish and seafood. Modern ingredients and methods, along with recipes to delight even the most finicky eaters, make this book a great "catch" for any home chef.

Company's Coming
COOKBOOKS

Quick
&
Easy
Recipes

Everyday
Ingredients

Canada's
most popular
cookbooks!

Kitchen Tested
Company's Coming
Guaranteed Great!™

Complete your Original Series Collection!

- ❏ 150 Delicious Squares
- ❏ Casseroles
- ❏ Muffins & More
- ❏ Salads
- ❏ Appetizers
- ❏ Cookies
- ❏ Pasta
- ❏ Barbecues
- ❏ Preserves
- ❏ Chicken, Etc.
- ❏ Cooking For Two
- ❏ Slow Cooker Recipes
- ❏ Stir-Fry
- ❏ Make-Ahead Meals
- ❏ The Potato Book
- ❏ Low-Fat Cooking
- ❏ Stews, Chilies & Chowders
- ❏ Fondues
- ❏ The Beef Book
- ❏ The Rookie Cook
- ❏ Rush-Hour Recipes
- ❏ Sweet Cravings
- ❏ Year-Round Grilling
- ❏ Garden Greens
- ❏ Chinese Cooking
- ❏ The Beverage Book
- ❏ Slow Cooker Dinners
- ❏ 30-Minute Weekday Meals
- ❏ School Days Lunches
- ❏ Potluck Dishes
- ❏ Ground Beef Recipes
- ❏ 4-Ingredient Recipes
- ❏ Kids' Healthy Cooking
- ❏ Mostly Muffins
- ❏ Soups
- ❏ Simple Suppers
- ❏ Diabetic Cooking
- ❏ Chicken Now
- ❏ Kids Do Snacks
- ❏ 30-Minute Rookie Cook
- ❏ Low-Fat Express
- ❏ Choosing Sides
- ❏ Perfect Pasta And Sauces
- ❏ 30-Minute Diabetic Cooking
- ❏ Healthy in a Hurry
- ❏ Table for Two NEW Feb. 1/09

FREE Online NEWSLETTER

- **FREE** recipes & cooking tips
- **Exclusive** cookbook offers
- **Preview** new titles

Subscribe today!

www.companyscoming.com

COLLECT ALL Company's Coming Series Cookbooks!

Most Loved Recipe Collection
- ❏ Most Loved Barbecuing
- ❏ Most Loved Salads & Dressings
- ❏ Most Loved Casseroles
- ❏ Most Loved Stir-Fries
- ❏ Most Loved Holiday Favourites
- ❏ Most Loved Slow Cooker Creations
- ❏ Most Loved Summertime Desserts
- ❏ Most Loved Festive Baking NEW November 1/08

3-in-1 Cookbook Collection
- ❏ Meals Made Easy

2-in-1 Cookbook Collection
- ❏ Healthy Choices
- ❏ The Rookie Cook's Companion NEW January 1/09

Lifestyle Series
- ❏ Diabetic Dinners
- ❏ Healthy in a Hurry
- ❏ Whole Grain Recipes

Special Occasion Series
- ❏ Christmas Gifts from the Kitchen
- ❏ Timeless Recipes for All Occasions
- ❏ Christmas Celebrations
- ❏ Cooking at Home
- ❏ Company's Coming—Tonight! NEW October 1/08

Practical Gourmet
- ❏ Small Plates for Sharing NEW September 1/08

Cookbook Author Biography
- ❏ Jean Paré: An Appetite for Life

Canada's most popular cookbooks!